Marquart's Works

VOLUME
IV

APOLOGETICS

Edited by
Herman J. Otten

LUTHERAN NEWS, INC., New Haven, Missouri

Marquart's Works

Library of Congress Card
Lutheran News, Inc.
684 Luther Lane
New Haven, MO 63068
Published 2014
Printed in the United States of America
Lightning Source, Inc., La Vergne, TN
ISBN #978-0-9644799-8-2

TABLE OF CONTENTS

FOREWORD

Dr. Marquart was a beloved Professor by all the students that sat in his classes. His ability to simplify great theological concepts made him a favorite Teacher for all the students who attended the Seminary. He not only instilled in us a love for Theology, but he also showed us how it was to be applied in a pastor's daily calling.

However, these writings are not just for pastors. Even dedicated laymen will be able to grasp and learn from this great Teacher of the Church. Whenever and wherever Dr. Marquart made a presentation, you would soon see that he was eagerly sought out, not just by pastors but also by laymen. They too recognized his genius in refuting those who denied the Word of God. He was as popular with laymen as he was with pastors. Here in these volumes you will once again be able to take your place and listen to this great Teacher, as he clearly enunciates various topics from a thoroughly Lutheran perspective. Since these multiple volumes consist of the various topics that Dr. Marquart addressed over his illustrious life, you will find it hard to put these volumes down.

Having Dr. Marquart's writings in book form will once again allow this fearless Champion of the Church to speak to the issues that continue to plague the Church from one generation to the next. False doctrine continues to be rehashed and sent out with new clothes. As the Proverb goes, "there is nothing new under the sun." Dr. Marquart had the remarkable ability to dissect what the issue was, and why it was, and still is, false doctrine. Confessional Lutherans from all over the world were always eager to attend Dr. Marquart's lectures. They recognized that he was a giant among men. Anyone concerned about the welfare of the Church will want to have these volumes on their bookshelf.

It appears that the Almighty Savior of the Church, in His infinite wisdom, chooses to send out only a few Teachers of the Church. One may make a very short list of these esteemed gifts from God. Luther, Chemnitz, Gerhard, Walther, Pieper, Preus, and Marquart. Their writings stand the test of time. These men did not write for some passing fad, that is here today and then blown away by tomorrow's changing wind vane. Any pastor or layman, who has a desire and love for the Truth, will not be disappointed with these volumes. Every congregation that has a love for the Lord and His saving Gospel, would do well to purchase the writings from these Teachers of the Church. God had His good reasons for raising these men up and sending them out, and it would be wise for pastors and laymen to read, mark, learn and inwardly digest the writings of these great defenders of the Gospel.

Rev. Herman Otten is to be commended for publishing the writings of Dr. Kurt Marquart. This may well be Rev. Otten's finest and most enduring contribution to the Church.

Rev. Ray R. Ohlendorf
Salem Lutheran Church
Taylorsville, NC
4th Sunday in Lent 2014

i

Acknowledgements

Well Herman,

As usual you find yourself doing what unsere beliebte Synode should have done long ago. The fact that CPH has not already published a book of Kurt's writings is an absolute travesty. It is an indictment of the politics before theology which has destroyed the orthodoxy of the LCMS. Our Savior Lutheran Church will stand by you in the worthy project. Back in the dark days when Bohlmann and his supporters were after Robert Preus we published a number of Kurt's magnificent essays on Robert's behalf. Modern Missouri has never produced another theologian comparable to him either in confessional fidelity or eloquence. We are proud and eager to take part in this belated effort. "Gottes Wort Und Luthers Lehr Vergehet Nun Und Nimmermehr."

Larry White, Pastor
Our Saviour Lutheran Church
Houston, Texas

Thanks to Luke Otten for arranging the publication of these volumes and to Naomi Finck, John Eberhart, Natalie Hoerstkamp, and Mary Zastrow for type-setting.

Thanks to Grace Otten for recognizing the importance of publishing *Marquart's Works* ever since they first began appearing in *Christian News* more than 50 years ago. Thanks to Scott Meyer, "America's confessional Lutheran" lay historian and President of the Concordia Historical Institute whose appreciation of Marquart's works and encouragement helped make the publication of these volumes possible.

PREFACE

Dr. C. F. W. Walther, first president of The Lutheran Church-Missouri Synod, has been rightly referred to as "The American Luther." As the editor of a Christian weekly for 51 years, the undersigned has reviewed thousands of books. During all these years he has published the writings of many theologians. The index at the back of Volume V of the *Christian News Encyclopedia* lists the names of hundreds of theologians whose writings have appeared in *Christian News*. Some, like Kurt Marquart, were also good friends. Yet, the editor knows of no theologian who deserves the title "The International Lutheran" more than Kurt Marquart. The editor's wife, Grace, is a graduate of Concordia College, St. Paul Minnesota and Valparaiso University. There she studied under some prominent theologians who later became professors at Concordia Seminary, St. Louis and Seminex. In 1963 Grace Otten and Kurt Marquart were *CN*'s reporters at the Fourth Assembly of the Lutheran World Federation in Helsinki, Finland. Following the LWF Assembly she and the editor's brother, Walter, who knew Marquart for 54 years, accompanied him on a twenty city lecture tour in the U.S. Grace shares the editor's evaluation of Kurt Marquart. She helped make it possible together with Luke Otten, Ruth Rethemeyer, Mary Beth Otten, Kristina Bailey and the Missourian Publishing Company, Washington, Missouri, to get *Marquart's Legacy* published in 2006 not long after his death. The 76 page *Marquart's Legacy* is available from *Christian News* for $5.00. It includes photos of Marquart and family and information about two professionally made videos showing Marquart in action.

Marquart's Legacy begins with a brief biography of Kurt Marquart. Then follows "Remembrances of a Former Seminary Roommate," the editor of *Christian News*. Next comes "The Lasting Legacy of Kurt Marquart" as expressed by many who knew him well.

The appendixes list the writings and reports of Kurt Marquart which have appeared in 44 volumes of *Christian News* (1962-2006), *A Christian Handbook on Vital Issues*, the five volumes of the *Christian News Encyclopedia, Luther Today, What Would He Do or Say?* and *Crisis in Christendom-Seminex Ablaze*. The lasting legacy of a great theologian and genius like Kurt Marquart can best be found in his works. *CN* suggested in 2006 that the Lutheran Church-Missouri Synod's Concordia Publishing House should publish *Marquart's Works*.

The questions at the end of each section are included to make *Marquart's Works* helpful for study. In an age when faith in historic Christianity is declining in all of the major denominations, *Marquart's Works* can be used to encourage and strengthen faithful Christians and begin a 21st Century Reformation and 21st Century Formula of Concord by the 500th anniversary of the Reformation in 2017.

Herman Otten
Reformation, 2014

THE CASE AGAINST EVOLUTION

(The original version of the following article appeared, as one of several contributions on the subject, in the December, 1965, issue of the LUTHERAN STUDENT, mimeographed at the University of Adelaide. LUTHERAN NEWS asked me to remove a few references to the original context of the debate, so as to make a general article out of the item. K.M.)

There are two assumptions which seem to me to underlie most "religious" treatments of evolution nowadays: (1) that evolution is genuinely scientific, and (2) that it is theologically neutral, no more incompatible with Christianity than, say gravity. Neither of these assumptions seems tenable to me.

I. Evolution as Science

I have studied this question with great interest for more than a decade, and certain things have become increasingly clear to me. I do not of course lay claim to anything more that amateur status in the field of science. I do think it self-evident however that just as the lawyer can acquire a competent understanding of some technical point relating to his case, even to the extent of being able to discomfit hostile expert witnesses, so the educated Christian can and must make responsible decisions in any field of specialization which impinges upon the Faith.

I submit four lines of argument from fact to show that evolution is not a scientific fact but a metaphysical opinion:

Competent Scientists

(1) Not only theologians but competent scientists themselves question or reject the scientific status of evolution.

The 1937 edition of the ENCYCLOPEDIE FRANCAISE (V, 82-87) contains an essay, "What Are the Theories of Evolution Worth?" by Paul Lemoine, Director of the National Museum in Paris. Excerpts follow:

> The theories of evolution with which our studious youth have been deceived constitute actually a dogma that all the world continues to teach; but each in his specialty, the zoologist or the botanist, ascertains that none of the explanations furnished are adequate...It results from this summary that the theory of evolution is impossible...But evolution is a sort of dogma which the priests do not believe, but maintain for their people...it is necessary to have the courage to say this, so that men of a future generation may orientate their researches in a different direction.

It seems that France never accorded Darwinism that ready credulity with which was acclaimed in the Anglo-Saxon world. In fact, the French Academy originally refused to receive Darwin into membership, because, as a prominent member of the Academy pointed out in LES MONDES, Darwin's most famous book, THE ORIGIN OF SPECIES and particularly THE DESCENT OF MAN, are "not science, but a mass of assertions and absolutely gratuitous hypotheses, often evidently fallacious. This kind of publication and these theories are a bad example, which a body that respects itself cannot encourage."

In his Introduction to the Everyman's Library centenary edition of the ORIGIN, W.R. Thompson, F.R.S., Director of the Commonwealth Institute of Biological Control at Ottawa, has written:

> I am not satisfied that Darwin proved his point or that his influence in scientific and public thinking has been beneficial...since no one has explained to my satisfaction how evolution could happen I do not feel impelled to say that it has happened...As we know, there is a great divergence of opinion among biologists, not only about the causes of evolution but even about the actual process. This divergence exists because the evidence is unsatisfactory and does not permit any certain conclusion. It is therefore right and proper to draw the attention of the non-scientific public to the disagreements about evolution. But some remarks of evolutionists show that they think this is unreasonable. This situation, where scientific men rally to the defense of a doctrine they are unable to define scientifically, much less demonstrate with scientific rigor, attempting to maintain its credit with the public by the suppression of criticism and the elimination of difficulties, is abnormal and undesirable in science.

Dr. Heribert Nilsson, Professor of Botany in the University of Lund, published, in 1954, his 1300 page SYNTHETISCHE ARTBILDUNG (Artificial Speciation), in which he reported the results of his life's work in genetics and related fields. His conclusion:

> The final result of all my investigations and study, namely that the idea of evolution, tested by experiments in speciation and allied sciences, always leads to incredible contradictions and confusing consequences on account of which the evolution theory ought to be entirely abandoned, will no doubt enrage many; and even more so my conclusion that the evolution theory can by no means be regarded as an innocuous natural philosophy, but that it is a serious obstruction to biological research. It obstructs – as has been repeatedly shown – the attainment of consistent results, even from uniform experimental material. For everything must ultimately be forced to fit this speculative theory. An exact biology cannot therefore be built up.

Professor Henry M. Morris, Head of the Department of Civil Engineering in the Virginia Polytechnic Institute, put it like this in his recent (1963) book: *THE TWILIGHT OF EVOLUTION:*

> In his own relatively small circle of acquaintances, the writer personally knows men with the Ph. D. degree in geology, in biology, in anthropology, physics, chemistry, astronomy, entomology, hydrology, mathematics, genetics, archeology, and other sciences – as well, of course, as numerous men with Ph.D.'s in engineering – who do not believe in evolution. There is obviously nothing in any of these sciences, therefore, that really compels their practitioners to accept the supposed 'fact' of evolution. The latter is nothing but a propaganda device which has been used – and very effectively – to awe people into accepting it (p. 85).

2

PALEONTOLOGY

(2) It has never been shown that evolution has in fact occurred. Paleontology is the relevant scientific discipline here, because it deals with the only "documentary" evidence of the biological history of this planet, the fossils. Darwin himself was distressed by the fact that the fossil record indicates not an unbroken chain or continuity of forms, but a series of stubbornly isolated links without transitional forms. The principal taxonomic groups appear suddenly, fully developed and, like Melchizedek, without a trace of ancestry in supposedly "older" fossiliferous strata! This phenomenon is particularly glaring in the case of the flowering plants, whose sudden and massive appearance in the "middle cretaceous" period Darwin called an "abominable mystery." A hundred years ago it was confidently hoped that all the needed transitional forms would still be discovered. That hope has not been realized. Why is it that just the transitional forms required by evolution are regularly absent? Did the rocks have a bias against preserving them? Today this is generally explained by assuming that the transitional forms were few in number. But this is unscientific special pleading, on the maxim: "These are the conclusions upon which I have based my facts." It is as Darwin's friend and supporter T.H. Huxley, once admitted: The fossil evidence, honestly consulted about the evolutionary notions, "negatives" them!

Moreover, the various fossil-bearing strata do not, in nature, occur in the invariable simple-to-complex order required by the theory. The whole grandiose geologic time-scale is a purely theoretical construct read into rather than out of the rocks. First the rocks are arranged into an artificial time-sequence on the assumption that the "simple" fossils preceded the "complex" ones, and then this arbitrary scheme is used to "prove" the relative ages of the fossils! That this is really reasoning in a circle is admitted by the Cambridge scientist R.H. Rastall in the 1956 ENCYCLOPEDIA BRITANNICA ("Geology," vol. 10, p. 168).

Another remarkable circumstance is the luxuriant richness and variety of early life indicated by the fossil record. There were many more species and many organisms were much larger than representatives of the same species today. Indeed, our present-day flora and fauna seem pale and paltry by comparison. Frightful impoverishment, not improvement – devolution, not evolution – is the real lesson of the rocks. This makes good sense in the light of my fourth point below.

GENETICS

(3) It has never been shown that evolution is even possible in principle. The relevant discipline here is the science of genetics, which deals with heredity.

Darwin himself insisted that the evolution theory was valueless unless the cause or mechanism of evolution could be explained. In his ORIGIN OF SPECIES Darwin thought he had provided the explanation, i.e. natural selection acting on individual differences.

But the facts and interpretations on which Darwin relied have now

3

ceased to convince. The long-continued investigations on heredity and variation have undermined the Darwinian position. We now know that the variations determined by environmental changes – the individual difference regarded by Darwin as the material on which natural selection acts – are not hereditary (W.R. Thompson, F.R.S., in the Introduction to Darwin's ORIGIN OF SPECIES, Everyman's Library edition, 1959, p.xii).

Modern genetics, found on the work of the monk Gregory Mendel, knows what Darwin didn't know; that the offspring cannot inherit the parents' acquired characters. As a result Neo-Darwinism is forced to regard mutations as providing the variations on which natural selection acts. But this is particularly awkward, because mutations are destructive, not constructive. They are "mistakes" in the duplication of genes, i.e. the complex molecules which embody the "code" which determines the organism's heredity. One can understand how "mistakes" in this biochemical code can change or even eliminate existing structures and organs but it is impossible to account for the origin of new and useful organs in this manner. That would be like saying that the modern jetliner was developed by a series of accidental damages sustained by various parts of the original Wright brothers' flying machine! Mutations are essentially injuries, and are nearly always harmful, and usually lethal. They are about as likely to improve an organism as random hammer blows are likely to improve a delicately balanced machine. To suggest that man has developed from something like an amoeba by an accumulation of accidental injuries is so absurd as to border on the insane. Yet evolutionists have so far been unable to suggest any alternatives to the wretched mutations.

Each species simply has a certain variability curve within which varieties may be developed by selective breeding. As breeders of race-horses, dairy cattle, wheat, maize, etc., know, the variation cannot be continued indefinitely. It stops when a certain limit has been reached. And that happens within a few generations. Left to itself, the organism will perpetuate itself along a hereditary mean, about which the variations oscillate. Thus modern genetics knows of variety within the species, but not of any transformation of one species into another.

Very significant is the fact that it is actual experimental evidence, in other words, genuine science, which contradicts evolutionary speculations. That evolution is not merely a harmless hypothesis, but a positive obstacle in the path of true scientific work and progress, is maintained, for instance, by the late Lund University geneticist, Heribert Nilsson, and the eminently successful horticulturist, Dr. W. Lammerts (Ph.D., Genetics). The latter is Director of Research, Germain Horticultural Research Division, Livermore, California and is known as the "father of scientific rose-breeding." He developed, among others, the award-winning "Queen Elizabeth Rose."

4

(4) The fundamental, and fatal, fallacy of evolution lies in its utter disregard of the Laws of Thermodynamics which are among the most basic and certain conclusions in all of science.

Take the First Law (Conservation). From it we would infer that since the observable universe is not now being created, it must have originated by entirely different processes and forces than those now in operation. But evolution assumes the uniformitarian dogma that all present-day phenomena can and must be accounted for solely in terms of forces and processes observable now. If we were to try this reasoning in the case of, say, an old cathedral, we would have to conclude about like this: The cathedral must be accounted for in terms of forces and processes now seen to be operating in or on it. It is obvious; therefore, that climatic conditions, weekly preaching and singing, weddings and funerals, the burning of candles, bird-deposits, etc., gradually formed the cathedral! We cannot assume a builder, stonemasons, etc., because none are now to be seen about the cathedral! By exactly the same logic evolution teaches the self-development of everything from nothing, by means of no other forces than those now in operation.

According to the Second Law of Thermodynamics, any system, let to itself, will deteriorate, not improve; that is, it will become more and more random, less and less complex and organized. No exception to this rule has ever been observed. But according to the unproved notion of evolution, everything is constantly getting less and less random, and more and more organized and highly developed! The Second Law of Thermodynamics – a generalization based on the widest possible experience – teaches that, left to itself, a building will tend to turn into a pile of rubble, not the other way around. But evolution holds that a pile of inorganic rubble has, in fact turned not merely into cathedrals, but into the infinitely more complex beings who plan and build them!

Julian Huxley, in his introduction to de Chardin's grandiose mythology, THE PHENOMENON OF MAN, naively confesses:

(Evolution) "is an anti-entropic process, running counter to the second law of thermodynamics with its degradation of energy and its tendency to uniformity. With the aid of the sun's energy, biological evolution marches uphill, producing increased variety and higher degrees of organization."

The Laws of Thermodynamics are solid, verified science, evolution is not.

EVOLUTION AS THEOLOGY

It is very clear, I think, that evolution is a metaphysical, not a scientific theory. Its inner dynamic has more to do with historical, psychological, even spiritual forces, than with empirical facts. And I cannot see how the philosophical dogmas of evolution can be harmonized with Christianity except at the cost of jettisoning the latter's foundations:

ESSENTIALLY ATHEISTIC

(1) Cosmic evolution – of which organic evolution is simply one aspect – is essentially a scheme by which the creature attempts – for obvious reasons, I think – to account for itself without reference to the Creator. Dr. W. Oesch uttered a profound truth, therefore, when he wrote that the theory of evolution is fundamentally and essentially atheistic. He was not of course referring to such trivialities as the subjective, and inconsistent, states of mind of individuals trying to follow both Christ and Darwin; rather, he was making a significant assertion about the objective locus of evolution in history and philosophy. Dr. D. M. S. Watson's famous statement, of 1929, to the British Association is to the point: "Evolution is a theory universally accepted, not because it can be proved to be true, but because the only alternative, 'special creation' is clearly impossible."

Compromise with the evolutionary scheme puts one on the inclined plane which inevitably leads to the atheology of Robinson and his ilk.

UNDERMINES REDEMPTION

(2) Evolution negates the Biblical doctrines of man and of sin, and thus undermines the doctrine of the Redemption. Evolution holds, of, course, not that an animal population suddenly, by saltation, produced two human beings, but that a human population developed gradually from the animals.

The theistic evolutionist must hold that somewhere along the line God infused human souls into what were animals before. Now, there are two alternatives. Either God gave souls to only two anthropoid creatures, or else He gave them the whole population. If the former, then many people today might not have souls, since they would be descendants of the soulless anthropoids, which would have been physically indistinguishable from the "souled pair." (To introduce a salutatory physiological difference at the moment of infusion of the soul is to undo the very "scientific" stance for the sake of which one accepted evolution in the first place! Darwin: "I would give absolutely nothing for the theory of natural selection, if it required miraculous additions at any stage of descent.") But if a whole anthropoid population received souls and became homo sapiens, then mankind's unity of origin and "solidarity in sin" are undetermined. Or how does one make sense of the Fall and original sin on the theory of a whole population of "Adams" and "Eves"?

And that the Christian doctrines of the Person and Office of Christ collapse when the supporting doctrines of Biblical anthropology and hamartiology are withdrawn, is evident both a priori, from logic, and a posteriori, from the example of modern theology, which accepts neither a real Incarnation, nor a real Atonement.

A QUESTION OF IDOLATRY

(3) The popular modern "interpretation" of Genesis necessarily rests on a conception of revelation which is perfectly consistent with Liberal assumptions but totally incompatible with any serious commitment to the teaching authority of Christ and His Apostles.

6

The real issue is not of course our right to prescribe God's mode of creation, but His right to prescribe our belief about His creation! This divine right no orthodox Christian will deny.

But the religious Liberal has no such inhibitions. He approaches Genesis without even expecting to be told any facts to be accepted on authority. For the whole realm of fact has been unconditionally surrendered to "science," and theology banished to a remote limbo whence only "values" and "meanings" are permitted to ooze out upon reality! Genesis therefore is a priori forbidden to teach any real, specific facts about how this universe or mankind did or did not come into being. Only "science" is competent to supply such information. The Liberal, before ever consulting Genesis, already "knows" from "science" that evolution is the answer. All that remains to be done is to find in Genesis suitable "meanings" or "theological interpretations" with which to sprinkle the established "facts" of "science," without of course in any way contradicting them. In case of conflict, "science" must always have the right of way.

Nor is the New Testament allowed to appear in behalf of Genesis. Its testimony is from the outset regarded as irrelevant, incompetent, and immaterial to determination of the original and true meaning of Genesis. The "interpretations" given by Christ and His Apostles were based on a pre-scientific worldview, and do not bind us in terms of fact. Contemporary pagan "literary forms" are treated as a far safer index to the real meaning of Genesis, that the "dogmatic" pronouncements of the New Testament.

The Christian interpreter on the other hand must proceed quite differently. He too will not rashly exclude the possibility of figurative elements, also in Genesis – particularly in view of the exegetical work of some of the great Church Fathers of antiquity, who certainly believed in the inviolable authority of Holy Writ. Nor will he needlessly dogmatize about scientific details, or assume that Scripture provides a host of easy answers, which render rigorous, disciplined scientific research and cogitation superfluous. But the Christian interpreter will bind himself in advance to the proper, intended sense of Genesis no matter who or what may contradict it. He will also accept as a certainty, from the outset, that Christ and His inspired Evangelists and Apostles had the correct understanding of Genesis. If therefore Christ and Apostles accepted the Creation and Fall narratives at face value – as they clearly did in St. Matthew 19:3-6, St. Luke 3:38, Romans 5:12-19, I Corinthians 11:7-9, and I Timothy 2:13-25, which treat Adam and Eve not as legendary, epic, or even "symphonic" (!) (all simply polite but increasingly desperate terms for "mythological" or "fictitious"!) characters, but as actual, real people – then every other possibility, no matter how plausible otherwise, is automatically ruled out and cannot be entertained.

To treat the case as open after Christ and His Apostles have rendered their verdict is to assure that they might have been in error. But this assumption is not a minor "exegetical problem," but a major attack upon the Lordship and teaching authority of Christ, and subverts the whole Christian religion. It is impossible to worship Christ as God's Word and

7

Truth Incarnate, and at the same time to be ashamed of His words (St. Mark 8:38); to believe him about "heavenly things", (St. John 3:12 to "cast down imaginations and every high thing that exalteth itself against the knowledge of God, and bringing into captivity every thought to the obedience of Christ" (II Corinthians 10:5), and still to prefer pseudo-scientific imaginations and high things to clear teachings of those of whom Christ said: "He that heareth you, heareth Me" (St. Luke 10:16), and: "If they have kept My saying, they will keep yours also" (St. John 15:20)!

The real issue then is not simply some innocent little "hermeneutical problem," whether Genesis is this or that kind of literary form, etc. The fundamental question is whether twentieth century Christians are really willing to affirm that Christ is Lord, and know what that means, or whether they are prepared to mumble "Lord, Lord," while negotiating compromises with the pseudo-scientific, naturalistic, anti-Christian, and even anti-theistic world-view of our time. Ultimately, it is a question of idolatry.

(Luther Today, What Would He Do and Say? Editor Herman Otten, pp. 168- 171)

Christian News, December 12, 1966

1. Is evolution scientific? ____.
2. Why did the French Academy originally refuse to admit Darwin? ____.
3. What does the fossil record indicate? ____.
4. Who did Darwin call an "abominable mystery?" ____.
5. What did Cambridge scientist R.H. Rastall admit was reasoning in a circle? ____.
6. The lesson of the rocks is ____ not ____.
7. Modern genetics has found that the offspring cannot inherit ____.
8. Mutations are ____ not constructive.
9. Does modern genetics know of any transformation from one species into another? ____.
10. Dr. W. Lammerts is known as ____.
11. Old cathedrals, according to the uniformitation dogma, were built by ____.
12. What is the Second Law of Thermodynamics? ____.
13. Evolution is a ____ not a scientific theory.
14. Dr. W. Oesch insisted that evolution is fundamentally and essentially ____.
15. What was Dr. D. M. S. Watson's famous statement of 1929 to the British Association? ____.
16. Evolution undermines the doctrine of ____.
17. Evolutionists insist that the "interpretations" given by Christ and the apostles are based on ____.
18. Did Christ and the Apostles accept the Creation and Fall narratives at face value? ____.
19. The fundamental question is whether twentieth century Christians are really willing to affirm ____.

8

EVOLUTION: SOME SERIOUS
THEORETICAL FLAWS

A review by Kurt Marquart of A. E. Wilder Smith, D.Sc., Ph.D.,
Dr. es. Sc., F.R.I.C., MAN'S ORIGIN, MAN'S DESTINY (Wheaton:
Harold Shaw Publishers, 1968), 320 pp.

Among contemporary sacred cows evolution is a veritable matriarch. The occasional intrepid soul who not only has serious intellectual doubts about the evolutionary faith but actually voices them, is likely to be treated as if he had just been introduced as the local secretary of the Flat Earth Society!

Indeed this reviewer has seen it stated in print that evolution is a scientific fact just as firmly established as the fact that the earth is round. This of course is pure bluff, and rather uninformed bluff at that. The simple fact of the matter is that while no educated person today holds to the idea of a flat earth, or entertains the slightest doubts on the subject, evolution continues to be questioned and even rejected by a number of qualified scientists and other informed thinkers.

It will be well to establish this point firmly in terms of explicit quotations, so that Professor Smith's arguments may receive a more open-minded hearing than they are likely to get otherwise.

Professor Henry Morris, Ph.D., is Head of the Department of Civil Engineering at the renowned Virginia Polytechnic Institute and is a fellow of the American Association for the Advancement of Science.

He writes:

> "In his own relatively small circle of acquaintances, the writer personally knows men with the Ph.D. degree in geology, in biology, in anthropology, physics, chemistry, astronomy, entomology, hydrology, mathematics, genetics, archaeology, and other sciences-as well; of course, as numerous men with Ph.D.'s in engineering-who do not believe in evolution. There is obviously nothing in any of these sciences; therefore, that really compels their practitioners to accept the supposed 'fact' of evolution. The latter is nothing but a propaganda device which has been used and very effectively-to awe people into accepting it." (TWILIGHT OF EVOLUTION, p. 85).

Dr. W. R. Thompson, F.R.S., Director of the Commonwealth Institute of Biological Control, Ottawa, Canada has contributed a fascinating introduction to the Everyman's Library centenary edition of Darwin's ORIGINS OF SPECIES (London: J.M. Dent & Sons; New York: E. P. Dutton & Co., 1958). Taking issue with the laudatory introduction written twenty-five years earlier by Sir Arthur Keith, Thompson casually drops little bombs like these:

> "I am not satisfied that Darwin proved his point or that his influence in scientific and public thinking has been beneficial" (p. vii).

> "I am of course well aware that my views will be regarded by many biologists as heretical and reactionary. However, I happen to believe

9

that in science heresy is a virtue and reaction often a necessity, and that in no field of science are heresy and reaction more desirable than in evolutionary theory" (IBID).

"But the facts and interpretations on which Darwin relied have now ceased to convince...the position therefore is that while the modern Darwinians have retained the essentials of Darwin's evolutionary machinery, to wit, natural selection, acting on random hereditary variations, their explanation, plausible in Darwin's day, is not plausible now" (pp. xii-xiii).

"Darwin himself considered that the idea of evolution is unsatisfactory unless its mechanism can be explained. I agree, but since no one has explained to my satisfaction how evolution could happen, I do not feel impelled to say that it has happened. I prefer to say that on this matter our information is inadequate" (p. xv).

"'As we know, there is a great divergence of opinion among biologists, not only about the causes of evolution but even about the actual process. This divergence exists because the evidence is unsatisfactory and does not permit any certain conclusion. It is therefore right and proper to draw the attention of the nonscientific public to the disagreements about evolution. But some recent remarks of evolutionists show that they think this unreasonable. This situation, where scientific men rally to the defense of a doctrine they are unable to define scientifically, much less demonstrate with scientific rigor, attempting to maintain its credit with the public by the suppression of criticism and the elimination of difficulties, is abnormal and undesirable in science" (p. xxii).

Heribert Nilsson, Professor of Botany in the University of Lund, Sweden, summarized his life's work in a 1000-page volume on artificial speciation. Here is his conclusion.

"The final result of all my investigations and study, namely that the idea of evolution, tested by experiments in speciation and allied sciences, always leads to incredible contradictions and confusing consequences, on account of which the evolution theory ought to be entirely abandoned, will no doubt enrage many; and even more so my conclusion that the evolution theory can by no means be regarded as an innocuous natural philosophy, but that it is a serious obstruction to biological research. It obstructs—as has been repeatedly shown—the attainment of consistent results, even from uniform, experimental material. For everything must ultimately be forced to fit this speculative theory. An exact biology cannot therefore be built up."

These recent statements of prominent scientists are only a few of the many that could be cited. They suffice completely, however, to brand as propaganda myth the hackneyed claim that "all educated people" accept evolution.

With these preliminaries out of the way, let us turn to Professor Smith's book, first of all noting the author's academic and scientific credentials. A. E. W. Smith studied natural sciences at Oxford University and in 1941 received his Ph.D. in organic chemistry from Reading University. From 1945 to 1949 he pursued cancer research at London's Middlesex Hospital Medical School, University of London. From 1951 to 1955 he held the position of Chief of Research at Geistlich Soehne (Pharmaceuticals), Ltd., at Lucerne, and in 1964 was granted the Doctor of Science degree from the University of Geneva. During the same year he received his third doctorate at the E.T.M. in Zurich Switzerland.

Prof. Smith has authored and co-authored more than 50 scientific publications and is widely known as a speaker to university student groups, both in Europe and in the U.S.A., on such subjects as recent advances in pharmacology, drug addiction, and Darwinism in contemporary thought.

Dr. Smith's wide university teaching experience includes his lectures on chemotherapy and pharmacology at the School of Medicine in Geneva from 1956 to 1964. While on leave from Geneva, he was visiting Professor of Pharmacology at the University of Illinois, at the Medical Center, Chicago, during 1957-1958, and visiting Professor of Pharmacology at the School of Medicine, University of Bergen, Norway, 1960-1962. Since 1964 he has been Professor of Pharmacology at the Medical Center, University of Illinois. He received the "Golden Apple" award for "the best course in five years of college life" from the senior students in the College of Pharmacy in 1967 and the same award from the School of Nursing in 1968. For three consecutive years, 1966, 1967, and 1968, he received the "Instructor of the Year" award and citation for the best senior year course. In a covering letter, students commented, "He made us not only better scientists, but better men."

Mathematicians, Computers, and Biologists

On pp. 218-223 we have a report of a discussion, held in Switzerland in 1965, between four mathematicians (Murray Eden, M.I.T.; S.M. Ulam, Los Alamos; V. Weisskopf, formerly director of CERN, Geneva, and now of M.I.T.; and M.P. Schutzenberger, University of Paris) and two biologists. A similar discussion was reported by Robert Bernhard (Assistant Editor) in "Heresy in the halls of biology: mathematicians question Darwinism," SCIENTIFIC RESEARCH, vol. 2, no. 11 (November, 1967), pp. 59 ff., and in SCIENCE, 160 (1968) pp. 408 ff. The complete transcript is available from the Wistar Institute Press, Philadelphia, as Wistar Institute Symposium Monograph No. 5, MATHEMATICAL CHALLENGES TO THE NEO-DARWINIAN INTERPRETATION OF EVOLUTION.

The mathematicians pointed out that chance variation or randomness, the very thing on which evolutionary dogma had relied for a hundred years, could not account for the bio-chemical complexities of life. For instance, Dr. Eden compared the number of proteins synthesized in nature with the vast number of possible protein molecules (10^{325}) and concluded that "out of all the possible paths, short and long, which evolution might have taken in establishing useful proteins, it has selectively moved along the shortest."

Dr. Schutzenberger analyzed Neo-Darwinian selection theory from a computer-mathematical viewpoint and concluded that "it is not conceivable."

Dr. Eden suggests that one of the principal tasks of evolutionists was "to relegate the notion of randomness of a minor and noncrucial role." Said Schutzenberger:

"Thus to conclude, we believe that there is a considerable gap in the neo-Darwinian theory of evolution, and we believe this gap to be of such nature that it cannot be bridged within the current conception of biology."

It is interesting to note the neo-Darwinians' response to these mathematical difficulties. They argued in effect that evolution was not subject to mathematical analysis (i.e. "quantification of biological measurements") and that mathematicians should leave it alone!

It was noted that biologists were "exquisitely sensitive" about any critical probing of neo-Darwinian theory. Of course, the probing went rather deep. Dr. Eden claimed that:

"concepts such as natural selection by the survival of the fittest are tautologous; that is, they simply restate the fact that only the properties of organisms which survive to produce offspring, or to produce more offspring than their cohorts will appear in succeeding generations."

To be meaningful, natural selection must offer "some rule of evolutionary behavior that can be tested." As it is, natural selection is so vague and general that it can be neither proved nor disproved—not to speak of the impossibility of devising a crucial experiment. Strictly speaking, therefore, the ruling evolutionary orthodox is, from the point of view of logical analysis, meaningless! That is why it can so easily and glibly be applied to almost any set of facts. Dr. Fentress (University of Rochester's Brain Research Center) for instance reported:

"I would simply like to give one example which I think illustrates how important it is to ask a precise question. When I was in Cambridge, we were working with two species of British vole (a kind of field-mouse. K.M.) We had a little test in which an object moved overhead; one species would freeze. Also, one species happened to live in the woods and the other happened to live in the field. This was rather fun, not really being a zoologist, I went up to see some of my zoologist friends and I reversed the data. I asked them, simply, why a species which lived in the field should freeze and why one that lived in the woods should run away (when the converse was the case). I wish I had recorded their explanations, because they were very impressive indeed."

In other words, natural selection can explain anything, even non-facts and anti-facts!

It may be interesting to note in this connection that this charge of tautology was brought, in a different form, already by Darwin's contemporary, Hooker, who wrote to Darwin that if all organisms that ever existed had survived and left offspring, all known forms of life would still have developed, and without any natural selection. Darwin had to agree!

A Clash with Basic Scientific Law

The basic trouble of course is that in nature order does not arise out of chaos by chance. Random processes lead not to order but to disorder. And this is probably the Achilles' heel of the whole Darwinian scheme. At this point evolution does not merely go beyond scientific fact, but actually contradicts it. For the principle that things left to themselves will tend to disorder, not of order, is one of the most apparent facts about our physical universe. It is known as the Second Law of Thermodynamics.

It will be objected, of course, that thermodynamics deals with the limited field of energy-conversions involving heat. It is true of course that the laws of thermodynamics were first elaborated a hundred years ago in connection with steam engines. It was found that although the total amount of energy in a closed system remained the same, the energy available for work decreased.

However, these principles have been found to have much broader implications. All known physical processes in the universe "run down," that is, tend toward a state of ever greater probability, randomness, and disorganization. In other words, piles of rocks, metals etc., do not tend to develop into cathedrals or spaceships, but, on the contrary, cathedrals or spaceships, left to themselves, tend to turn into piles of rocks and scrapmetal. Intelligently directed, purposive force is required to overcome and reverse the tendency toward disorder.

Evolution, however, holds, in defiance of the known nature of all physical reality, that a pile of inorganic minerals (the young earth in evolutionary science fiction) gradually produced, by random processes without any intelligent direction, not merely cathedrals and space-ships, but the vastly more intricate human beings who design and build them!

The usual objection at this point is that our argument applies only to closed or isolated systems, but that since our planet is continuously "open" to vast amounts of solar energy, the origin of life, although admittedly improbable, can be explained in harmony with the Second Law. Smith deals in some detail with this objection, and it is worth quoting him in full:

> A sardine can full of sardines hermetically sealed illustrates the nature of a closed system pretty well. As long as it is sealed, the "sardine molecules" will only slowly decompose and off-tastes will only slowly develop. Entropy will increase with time, the "sardine molecules" will decompose. If one now opens the can and inoculates the contents with penicillium notatum, for example, then something new will happen, if the conditions of temperature and moisture are right. The "sardine molecules" will be broken down by the penicillium notatum organism to supply energy to raw materials for new "penicillium molecules." Although in general, overall entropy will have been increased (more molecular order is in toto destroyed than synthesized), locally in the organism entropy will have been decreased and order increased.
>
> So the second law is only valid for isolated systems. As soon as outside energy exchanges (introduction of a living organism to the

13

sterile sardines) are permitted, at the cost of an overall general increase in disorder.

But if we increase the sardine can to the size of Switzerland and still keep it hermetically sealed and full of sardines, will new life appear in this sealed system? The answer is, of course, no, for the laws of the thermodynamics are not dependent on the size of the isolated system (the can) concerned. We go one step further. We increase the can size of our planet, still keeping it hermetically sealed and full of sardines. Will life appear in this large can spontaneously? The answer is, of course, again no—as long as the system really is isolated.

It is important to realize in using this example that the penetration of our "sardine can" (the whole isolated planet) by sunlight and cosmic radiation does not "open" it in the same way as we "opened" the sardine can to introduce pencillium notatum. For, as Dr. Blum has mentioned, the energy of sunlight cannot be used directly for molecular synthesis without the medium of a "motor." Sunlight cannot work on nonliving molecules of matter to yield organic synthesis, owing to the difficulty of summating its quanta. Just as the energy of petroleum cannot be conveniently used and harnessed without the intermediary of a properly designed internal-combustion or steam engine neither can sunlight properly quanta be used without a properly constructed photosynthetic motor, which is not present in nonliving matter, for reducing carbon dioxide to sugars and starch. Once more, the problem of providing a complex motor to utilize solar energy has to be solved. And such complex motors do not arise by chance from nonliving matter. This is basically the problem which Darwinists avoid or beg (p. 83).

The fantastically complex combinations of molecules required by and for life are of course admitted to be highly improbable events. But it is often argued that given enough time the virtually impossible becomes the virtually certain, that is, the most improbable events will occur sooner or later, if enough time is available.

Smith, however, points out that "the ordinary formula for increasing probability with time...does not apply to biological and chemical systems longer time for reaction gives increasing chance of equilibrium being established. That is, by increasing the time, the probability of the spontaneous formation of, for example, a hemoglobin molecule from simple organic chemicals, decreases—random equilibrium is favored" (p. 68).

The celebrated evolutionist Harold F. Blum, author of TIME'S ARROW AND EVOLUTION, is quoted in support:

"I think if I were rewriting this chapter (on the origin of life) completely, I should want to change the emphasis somewhat. I should want to play down still more the importance of the great amount of time available for highly improbable events to occur. One may take the view that the greater the time elapsed the greater should be the approach to equilibrium, the most probable state, and it seems that this ought to take precedence in our thinking over the idea that time

14

provides the possibility for the occurrence of the highly improbable."

Would Synthetic Life Disprove God?

Prof. Smith's answer is most effective:

It is commonplace reasoning today to assume that, because the biochemists are reputedly on the way toward synthesizing life in the laboratory, therefore God is explained away. The achievement of synthetic life is being awaited with gloating as the final nail in God's coffin. But is this reputable logic?

Every year I publish scientific articles on my synthetical experiments in leprosy and tuberculosis and report exact methods of synthesis and biological testing of the products. Assume now that a colleague reads my articles, finds the results interesting, and decides to repeat the work himself. After a year or so he finds all my methods exact (I hope!) and the biological activities of the synthetic products correct. He, in turn, reports his results in the scientific literature and in conclusion summarizes that he has repeated my experiments, found them correct and thereby exploded forever the myth of Wilder Smith's existence. I do not really exist at all, for he has been able to repeat my work! The logic is of course pretty well inconceivable! But yet it represents the actual position of the Darwinists and Neo-Darwinists today. For, man is on his way to thinking God's thoughts after him, repeating his work in the laboratory synthesis of molecules capable of bearing life. Man has "read" God's "publications" thoroughly in the study of the cosmos and nature, and is now verifying and repeating to some small degree his creative thoughts. We are coming up with "secondary" publications on results he has already achieved, and therefore the conclusion is drawn that, because of these secondary publications, God is a myth. He does not exist! We are not trying to prove the existence or nonexistence of God here, but merely the falsity of this kind of logic (pp. 92-93).

We might add: If indeed it should turn out to be the case that life can be "made" simply by arranging atoms or molecules in a certain way, it would follow not that life is any less miraculous, but that matter itself is far more miraculous than we suspected, in that it has a built-in potential for life!

What Difference Does it Make?

In a valuable appendix Prof. Smith reviews a number of relevant publications. The most interesting of these is THE IMPLICATIONS OF EVOLUTION (1960) by Dr. G. A. Kerkut, Professor of Physiology and Biochemistry in the University of South Hampton, and executive editor of the scientific journal COMPARATIVE BIOCHEMISTRY AND PHYSIOLOGY.

Dr. Kerkut isolates seven basic assumptions underlying evolution, and concludes that "in effect, much of the evolution of the major groups of an-

15

imals has to be taken on trust."

Readers may ask: Well what difference should it make to Christian thinkers whether evolution is true or not?

Leaving out of account the entire question of Biblical authority, it should be evident from the kind of material adduced by Dr. Smith that evolution is not so much science as philosophy. It is a particular belief or metaphysical opinion about the nature of the universe, i.e. that it is self-contained and can be explained without reference to any supranatural agency or intelligence. And from the point of view of Christian apologetics it does not of course make a great deal of difference whether the universe can be adequately accounted for without God or not. Christian thinkers will not want to swallow as scientific fact what is really a mere philosophical opinion, or to say it more pointedly, an anti-theistic prejudice!

One could go on to comment on many other valuable bits of information and argument from Prof. Smith's intriguing book. It contains, for instance, a discussion of the social and political consequences of Darwinism, an analysis of Oparin's theory of the origin of life, some interesting philosophical and theological speculations, and some photographs of fossils which must be regarded as positively obscene in the light of paleontological orthodoxy. But this review must end somewhere. Let it end with this quotation from Sir. James Jeans book THE MYSTERIOUS UNIVERSE, given on pp. 75-76 of Smith's:

> Nature seems very conversant with the rules of pure mathematics, as our mathematicians have formulated them in their studies, out of their own inner consciousness and without drawing to any appreciable extent on their experience of the outer world...IN the same way, a scientific study of the action of the universe has suggested a conclusion which may be summed up, though very crudely and quite inadequately, because we have no language at our command except that derived from our terrestrial concepts and experiences, in the statement that the universe appears to have been designed by a pure mathematician.
>
> ...the universe can be best pictured, although still very imperfectly and inadequately, as consisting of pure thought, the thought of what, for want of a wider word, we must describe as a mathematical thinker.
>
> There must have been what we may describe as a "creation" at a time not infinitely remote. If the universe is a universe of thought, then its creation must have been an act of thought...Modern scientific theory compels up to think of the creator as working outside time and space, which are part of his creation, just as the artist is outside his canvas...

Christian News, October 5, 1970

1. Among contemporary sacred cows, evolution is ____.
2. Are there scientists who reject evolution? ____.
3. How did Heribut Nilson summarize his life's work on artificial spe-

16

cialization? ____.

4. How many earned doctorates did A.E. Wilder Smith have. ____.

5. The ruling evolutionary orthodoxy is, from the point of logical analysis,

____.

6. What is the Achilles heal of the whole Darwinian scheme? ____.

7. What is the Second Law of Thermodynamics? ____.

8. Piles of rocks, metals etc. do not develop into ____.

9. What does a can of sardines hermeneutically sealed illustrate? ____.

10. What kind of logic are Darwinists using who say God does not exist?

____.

11. Evolution is not so much ____ as ____.

12. Sir James Jean noted that the universe appears to have been designed by ____.

FROM PALEY TO DARWIN

The Lutheran, February 13, 1984. (Australia)

NEW SERIES OF ARTICLES FOR 1984

In this issue we begin a series of articles by Kurt Marquart, formerly pastor in Toowoomba, Queensland, and now Professor at Concordia Seminary, Ft Wayne, USA. In this first article he looks at reasons for the collapse of Paley's theology before the onslaught of Charles Darwin. 'Part of the reason for Paley's vulnerability was that he tried to prove too much. I don't think he saw as clearly as a Christian theologian should have seen, the limitations of human reason.' Other articles will deal with the Sacraments and the Church.

Our civilization is in deep crisis. Many are trying to figure out just where things went off the rails. Up to about 200 years ago, it was generally taken for granted, that since there was so much evidence for order in the world, for example in plants and animals and the way the solar system runs, it seemed basic to believe that behind all this order there must be a great mind, a great intelligence. Things did not fall into place just by chance. To my knowledge, that was questioned in our civilization only twice, in any major way. The first time, about 500 to 600 years before the birth of our Lord, Greek philosophies suddenly began to question everything. They had some very silly things to question. They questioned the whole mythology of Mt. Olympus, and all those funny overgrown human beings like Zeus and Venus frolicking on Mt Olympus. Greek science and Greek philosophy were born questioning these silly myths. As often happens, things went overboard. One of Luther's favorite sayings was that the world was like a drunken peasant—he is never in the middle of the road except on the way from one ditch to the other, and so the world ran from one extreme to the other.

Having rejected the silly superstitions of Greek mythology, early Greek philosophy fell into the opposite extreme of denying any supernatural thing altogether. For a while the materialists believed everything was simply a matter of atoms rushing about like billiard balls bouncing off each other. But it didn't take very long for the greatest Greek thinkers—Plato and Aristotle—to realize that this simply would not do. Both Plato and Aristotle had reasonably elevated ideas of God, at least as good an idea of God as any pagan could have. There must at least be some intelligence out there, they suggested: that's as much as you can expect.

THE AGE OF ENLIGHTENMENT

Then came the Christian era. For nearly 2000 years it was simply taken for granted that God made everything. The order in the world indicated an orderly intelligence behind it. The second time this was seriously challenged was after the Renaissance, particularly at the time of the so called rationalist enlightenment in the 18th century. Now a real crisis developed, because suddenly everything had to be questioned —

18

everything had to be run through what somebody has called the 'sausage machine of human reason'. Everything had to be run through that grinder, and if it didn't compute with human reason, if it couldn't adequately be explained by reason, it was discarded as so much superstition. Man had now come of age. He was mature and didn't need authorities from heaven. He could work out everything by himself, thank you very much.

DAVID HUME AND IMMANUEL KANT

The two great philosophers who undermined the traditional philosophical arguments which people took for granted were David Hume, the Scottish philosopher, and the German, Immanuel Kant.

Between them, they launched a sharp attack on the idea that you could, from common reason, reliably argue for God. In the 18th century, these arguments were pretty much in shambles, except for one. They couldn't quite get rid of the argument from design. They undermined the other arguments, but there was a strong impression that there was order in the world, that the world was not just random chaos but an orderly system. And that, even Immanuel Kant didn't quite get rid of, and didn't dare to attack head-on.

THEOLOGIAN AND PHILOSOPHER

There was a possibility left, and into that breach there sprang a great English theologian and philosopher, William Paley. Archdeacon Paley had an excellent education and returned to teach at Cambridge. One of the books for which he is best known is entitled *Natural Theology*. Paley's argument was to state in crisp, up-to-date, scientifically respectable language, the common sense argument that everybody had always believed but nobody had bothered to put into precise terms—not even Thomas Aquinas, the great medieval genius, who wedded old Aristotelian philosophy to Christian thought. Even he had not gone into it as carefully as Archdeacon William Paley. And he did it with such great simplicity, charm and elegance that his argument seemed virtually irrefutable. What was his argument?

THE EXAMPLE OF THE WATCH

He began with his famous example of a watch. He said, if you happen to be crossing the heath in Scotland at night, and you stub your foot on a stone, you don't bother to think about how that stone got there — it doesn't require an explanation. Stones obviously belong in that sort of place. No great order is needed. But if you came across a watch in that place, you would know immediately, even if you didn't see any footprints, that the thing was obviously contrived. It is a machine that is designed for some purpose. The parts are obviously coordinated and pre-arranged to work in a certain way. Nobody would ever think that this watch could have simply happened out there on the heath.

Paley reasoned, if nobody would accept this simple watch, without an intelligence behind it, how much more forceful is the argument in the animal and plant world! Paley left astronomy alone. In those days not much

19

was known *about* astronomy. Paley said, 'I don't regard it as very useful because we can't experiment with the sun, moon and stars. There is nothing you can do to them.' And in a classic phrase he says, their very simplicity is against them. Nowadays they are not so simple anymore.

INFLUENCE IN ENGLAND AND BEYOND

Paley's book, *Natural Theology,* published in 1802, had an enormous impact in the entire English-speaking world, and no doubt beyond. It brought about a different public mood in England from that in the rest of Europe. In France and Germany, where so called free-thinking was very much in fashion, things had gone very far and the public mood was really hostile to Christianity and to the Church. In England, it was Paley who, with that book, single-handedly created a climate of opinion in which educated people thought: Yes, it makes sense to believe that there is a God. The book was required reading at all British universities for at least, I think, 100 years. It became a standard text-book. Darwin himself said that it was his favorite book at university. He virtually memorized it.

The great significance of this book was, that whereas modern philosophy seemed to have successfully questioned God, and everything was up for grabs, Paley found an argument which somehow was able to draft science in the service of religion, to marshal the force of science against the critical, skeptical acids of philosophy and the doubt of philosophy. That is the great achievement of Paley. But just when it seemed to be completely victorious, and when everybody was convinced of it suddenly came the great crash.

'THE ORIGIN OF SPECIES'

In 1859 Charles Darwin wrote *The Origin of Species.* Somebody had sent him a manuscript and anticipated his theories, so he thought he'd better get it published. With Wallace he presented a joint paper before a learned society, receiving joint credit. Afterwards, everybody forgot about Wallace and remembered only Darwin.

The year 1859 was like an explosion. The real significance of Darwin was not in biology — biology today could entirely ignore Darwin without any loss—the real significance of Darwin was cultural and philosophical. His great claim to fame is that he demolished the one non-religious argument that was left for the existence of God. You could always believe in the Bible by faith. The great argument of Paley was that you didn't need the Bible to prove there is a God—common sense tells you that. Darwin's great achievement, for better or for worse, was that he demolished the one argument that could still be brought in favor of a common-sense case for Christianity. This is basically why Darwin was so attractive to the Victorian world, and the wider European world beyond his horizons, because he gave a perfect way out to liberate the European intelligentsia from what they regarded as a straightjacket of having to always come to this dead-end where you have to refer to God.

'DARWIN AND THE PROBLEM OF CREATION'

In a recent book by Neil Gillespie, *Darwin and the Problem of Creation* (Chicago University Press), the author says that Darwin's basic achievement is not really scientific — it is philosophical. Darwin took biology out of a creationist frame of reference and put it in a so-called positive frame, where there would be no more reference to God. That's the real point. This is why I believe the debate between Paley and Darwin is so crucial to our time. Our whole modern culture rests on this assumption that there is no good public argument for God.

Our modern culture has gone atheistic or agnostic and the idea is: Yes, you can believe in God, but God is some kind of private, emotional limbo. People may believe in God if they wish to, if they have this emotional preference, but there is no compelling reason, no scientific, common-sense ground for it. It is Darwin's book that, having got rid of the last good argument for God, precipitated the modern age where God is out of the public realm and becomes something in the closet that people can privately appeal to with their emotions, but has no place in the public realm.

DARWINISM - 'DEAD AND DECAYING'

Darwin's book was so successful and convincing that 100 years later, at the Darwin centenary celebrated at the Chicago University in 1959/1960, the direct descendant, the grandson of Thomas Huxley, Darwin's good friend who pushed the Darwinian theory, Sir Julian Huxley, said that Charles Darwin had removed the whole notion of God from the realm of rational discussion. Darwin had shown, he said, that all the order that appeared in nature, the marvelous way in which cats, dogs, cactuses and crocodiles, and all these other beasts and Australian bushflies were put together, is only an illusion of order, because actually natural selection did it. Blind chance, throwing up more and more variations, and a shortage of food, simply weeded out the ones less qualified, and so the types kept getting better and better, more adjusted to the ecology and to the food supply. No God was necessary. Nature did it all by herself without any foresight or wisdom.

Only a few years ago when I was going to school, this view seemed solidly entrenched and seemed to have won the victory. What was not realized is the fact that even while the fulsome centenary rouge was being smeared all over Darwinism at Chicago only a quarter of a century ago, under the rouge the body of Darwinian doctrine was dead and decaying.

A NEW TORN OF EVENTS

To me this is a fascinating thing, a most exciting and quite unpredictable new turn of events. After World War II something entirely new happened. That arose out of a discipline from which you wouldn't expect much — the humble discipline of signal transmission. Maybe some of you were involved in World War II precisely in signal transmission. I understand that one of the ways in which the Americans mystified the Japanese was by using, not some code that they could have broken with a machine, but by using the Navajo Indian dialect. Suddenly the Japanese heard this Navajo chatter on the wireless and couldn't make out what it was. There are very few people in the world who speak Navajo!

COMMUNICATIONS AND LIFE ITSELF

The problems of communication engineering during the War were how to disguise a message, how to code and decode. The problem was especially acute in connection with the Battle of Britain when Nazi missiles and bombs were falling all over the United Kingdom and the British anti-aircraft did not have the wherewithal to fire accurately at the invading aircraft or missiles. They shot down only about one in ten of the planes that were attacking. They handed the problem over to American engineers and this is really the origin, I understand, of much of the modern computer world and of modern information theory in which the thing is grounded. Out of the need for this very practical need of calculating the flight path of an enemy aircraft, there came a discipline of how to calculate that. Once the Americans worked out a machine with an automatic gunsight, they began to shoot down 50 or 60 per cent of the incoming missiles. Out of this very practical discipline comes some surprisingly far-reaching results. One of the great things directly connected with this is the discovery that life itself could be related to the communications theory.

ALL THE LANGUAGE OF LIFE

The successful unravelling to some extent of the mystery at the basis of all biological life came in 1953 with the discovery of the DNA molecule (which is short for deoxyribonucleic acid). Francis Crick and James Watson won the Nobel Prize in 1953 for unravelling that molecule. It works like a computer tape, only instead of electronic magnetic charges, it works with biochemical coding. These chemical units are so sophisticated. They not only spell out messages; they even have signs for the beginning and ending of messages. With this highly complex, very sophisticated information system, you can spell out all the language of life, everything from cactus to peanuts, whales and humans. Everything you can think of is based on this biochemical computer code.

This has made an enormous impact on our whole way of perceiving living things because all of a sudden, guess what? Paley's watch is back. Only in much more intricate form! Paley's watch was a very primitive little machine. The one I have is a computer. This modern computerized watch flicks every split second. It is based on modern computing science. Nobody would believe that this complicated watch could have arisen simply from a metal scrapheap.

ENORMOUS CHANGE

The enormous change that this has brought about is that now suddenly everything becomes very problematical. How do you account for these complex living things, much more complicated than any computerized watch? Nobody believes that computers throw themselves together on a sunny afternoon. How can we account for living things throwing themselves or arising by accident? To me it is one of the ironies of history how gullible people can be, how gullible even the intelligentsia can be when it suits. Imagine if some major point of view were heavily tainted with Christian origins! There would be a lot of propaganda against it and people would say, 'Ah, yes, they got it from the Bible', or something like that. However, the modern view of the origin of life in some primeval soup — there is an old lagoon and the sun is shining for millions of years and gradually it thickens and some organic compound develops and in this organic soup something gradually happens, and some of it comes alive — this idea is taken from the Soviet scientist, Oparin, who calls it, by the way, much more appetizingly, bouillon — he says, this primeval bouillon turns out to be alphabet soup which then spells out this incredible complexity of all biological life. If you have ever tried to constrain alphabet soup to spell out a simple, silly digit like 'Happy birthday', you will not easily believe that that will do it by itself. But 'Happy birthday' is a very simple message compared to the kind of thing that human DNA imparts. It has been calculated that human DNA involves between 4000 and 5000 million separate pieces of information. Unimaginable!

A BOMBSHELL IS DROPPED

Recently a bombshell was dropped on this whole business, not by a biologist but by an astronomer. Paley thought astronomy didn't have much to offer, but at least astronomy taught man to think. The man I have in mind is Sir Fred Hoyle, a very great cosmologist, a renowned astronomer of the first rank, and a life-long atheist. During the 60s, he was the author of *The Steady State Theory of the Universe.*

He dropped a bombshell in 1981 at the Kellog Symposium in America when he said: The information content of the higher mammals, including human beings, can be represented by a figure of ten to the forty-thousandth power, which means 1 with 40,000 zeros behind it. You would have to produce a small book just to write that number! That is the information content represented in the higher mammals. And, he said, there is no way in the world that beings with that kind of information content could have arisen by random processes in our cosmos which is only, after all, some ten to the tenth power years old — about ten or twenty thousand million years. The disparity is so enormous that it is simply inconceivable, and Sir Fred added this, which amused me because I have always been using similar examples from the point of view of a childlike faith, but Sir Fred Hoyle said dogmatically, if you believe that, you may as well believe that a 747 jet could arise by a tornado striking a junk-yard, assembling it from the parts. I, for my part, can never see or understand the compulsion of biologists to deny what seems to me to be obvious.

"UP TO THE ULTIMATE LIMIT OF GOD"

Now he has written a book called *Evolution from Space,* where he believes that this enormous information content represented particularly by the human brain or human mind, is so impressive and so enormous

23

that it presupposes an order of intelligence much higher than any human. He is there suggesting something really that Francis Crick accepted. Remember, Francis Crick was the co-formulator of DNA. He studied as deeply as anybody how living cells really operate. For Francis Crick it became impossible to believe that life assembled on earth by accident.

Crick published a strange theory called Panspermia, in which he asserts that life got here, not by chance origin: it was brought here by a super civilization from outer space, that went about seeding the earth with various life forms! And he adds, probably from some sort of missionary motivation: 'I suppose they're out there now looking at the harvest, to see what might be done with it'. Hoyle is really suggesting some kind of super intelligence out there. But he is a little more sophisticated than Crick, because he says: 'A higher intelligence always presupposes a still higher one, up to the ultimate limit of God'. Coming from a life-long atheist, I think that is incredibly interesting. He is compelled to admit a series of intelligences 'up to the ultimate limit of God!' I find it much simpler to eliminate all these in-between occult speculations and to go directly to the ultimate limit of *God*. It is simpler and more elegant.

HISTORY GOES IN CYCLES

One thing that strikes me as ironic is that this whole way of thinking, which began with a denial of any necessity of God in the picture, has ended with back to primitive notions of God, the way we had them in ancient Greece. These sort of funny intelligences flying out there in flying saucers are really back to the level of Zeus and Venus and those people on Mt Olympus. By a strange twist of history, we with great intellectual effort, having sneered at superior notions of God, have barely begun to work our way back to the primitive, silly notions of ancient paganism. I wonder how long it will take before we think back up to the level of Plato and Aristotle and then consider whether the Bible doesn't have something to say to us. History goes in cycles like that.

INTELLECTUAL BUNK

My conclusion is that the kind of scientific atheism that has been confidently proclaimed for about 100 years, on which our modem *avante garde* cultural rejection of all Christian and traditional values has boastfully based itself, is thoroughly undermined today. It is known to be intellectual bunk. That has very serious consequences which I hope will begin to assert themselves also in our public life.

Christian News, June 25, 1984

1. Our civilization is in deep ____.
2. The two great philosophers who undermined the traditional philosophy were ____ and ____.
3. William Paley taught at ____.
4. Our whole modern culture rests upon the assumption that there is no ____.
5. Huxley said that Charles Darwin had removed ____.
6. DNA is short for ____.
7. Scientific atheism is thoroughly ____ today.

EVOLUTION COMING TO THE LCMS

"... the Synod needs to reassert effective doctrinal discipline within its Concordia University System. It appears that the old Seminex theology has its defenders here and there including open pro-evolutionism, together with a historical debunking of Genesis. Such things cannot go unchallenged without risking a total loss of the Word of God, as has happened in other American churches," Dr. Kurt Marquart of Concordia Theological Seminary, Fort Wayne, Indiana said in his address at the National Walther Conference held at Concordia Seminary, St. Louis on November 8, 2003.

"Putting Missouri Back on Track," the speech Dr. Marquart presented at the St. Louis Seminary was published in the November 17, 2003 Christian News. Parts of it together with an interview of Dr. Marquart are in the video "Crisis At The Crossroads" sent to all 6,000 LCMS churches.

When Dr. Marquart mentioned "open pro-evolution" in the LCMS's Concordia University System, one of the schools he had in mind was Concordia University, Portland. This issue of CN has several articles on the teaching of evolution at this school. A member of the school's Board of Regents is quoted as writing in a report to the Praesidium of the LCMS that Dr. Matthew Becker, a professor at Concordia Portland, who formerly taught at Concordia University, River Forest, Illinois, clearly denies the historicity of the Genesis account of creation and promotes evolution in his classroom teaching. LCMS President Jerry Kieschnick has been given the evidence but has done nothing. Becker continues to teach and Kieschnick has appointed Becker's attorney to the LCMS's CCM. The president of the Northwest District, who was a strong supporter of Seminex, protects Becker and anyone else in the Northwest District who promotes evolution. The Northwest District is rewarded by the LCMS's Nominating Committee by having 8 members of the district nominated by the committee for key positions in the LCMS. No other district was so highly honored.

Anyone who fails to recognize that evolution is coming into the LCMS with a roar simply does not know what is going on. Unfortunately, many do not care. CN is sending this issue of CN to all LCMS churches but many pastors, including those associated with organized conservative groups, never show the copy of Christian News which comes to their congregation to any members. Read in this issue: "DayStar Liberals Voice No Objection - BECKER AGAIN CALLS FOR ACCEPTANCE OF EVOLUTION IN LCMS," p. 1; "A Major Issue Facing 2004 LCMS Convention EVOLUTION, p. 9; "EVOLUTION IS NOT SCIENTIFIC," p. 10; "LCMS District Calls for Investigation of Concordia, Portland," p. 10; "Northwest District Defends Evolutionist," p. 11; "The Whole Church Is Christ's Mission: Education For Mission" by Matthew W. Becker, p.12; and "Science and Faith," p.14.

Some conservatives claim that evolution is not really a big threat in the LCMS because about the only one expressing any concern about the matter is the editor of Christian News. They claim that hardly any of the other conservative publications and websites in the LCMS have said much, if anything, about it. The "hyper-euro" conservatives often maintain that this is just another one of the "pet peeves" of an uncertified editor who can't get over what was going on in the LCMS when he was a student.

This issue of CN mentions some of the many books which CN has promoted for decades on creation and evolution. Dr. Alfred Rehwinkel, one of the editor's professors at Concordia Seminary, St. Louis, and his chief defender, is the author of The Flood (p. 1), published by Concordia Publishing House more than 50 years ago. It is still up to date and should be in the library of every LCMS pastor and church. During the Concordia Seminary vs. Otten case, Rehwinkel was Dr. Marquart's "Star Witness." Marquart was one of the editor's counselors who questioned both liberal and conservative professors who testified under oath before a board of 5 attorneys and 6 pastor-theologians. Rehwinkel knew that some of his fellow professors denied the inerrancy of the Bible and the historicity of the Genesis account of creation.

Dr. Erich von Fange is featured on page one. He is the author of several excellent books on creation which Concordia Publishing House should have published. They are all available from CN. Today there is no finer creationist in the LCMS than Dr. von Fange. He has taught at Concordia University, Seward; Concordia, Edmonton; and Concordia University, Ann Arbor.

Mention is also made in this issue of some excellent videos for both children and adults on creation. They should be widely used in all Christian day schools and homes. The many conservative publications and websites in the LCMS should be publishing if not selling these books and videos (p. 15).

This week the LCMS's Southwest District will sponsor a conference on theological issues. Among the speakers are Dr. Wallace Schulz, Dr. David Benke, Dr. Donald Matzat, Rev. Arthur Scherer, and Rev. Herbert Mueller.

Conservatives in the LCMS, who want to defeat Dr. Jerry Kieschnick, would get much further if they would hammer away at Kieschnick's tolerance of evolution in the LCMS than his simply granting Benke permission to pray with non-Christians. Many misdirected laymen still think it is wonderful that Benke used the words "Jesus" in his prayer at Yankee Stadium. Yet they want no part of evolution or women pastors in the LCMS.

If this editor were at the conference in Las Vegas where Benke will be speaking, he would ask: "Dr. Benke do you think the LCMS should be broad enough to allow its pastors and professors to teach that God used evolution to create man and the world, the first chapters of Genesis do not present historic fact, and women should be able to serve as pastor in the LCMS? The question is not what you personally believe but what you think should be tolerated in the LCMS." When Benke spoke at the DayStar conference in St. Louis where he again defended his prayer at

26

Yankee Stadium, CN asked whether such a question would be permissible. He was told by conference organizers: "NO!"

The overture published below is just one more effort to bring the matter of creation and evolution before another LCMS convention. The last time Trinity of New Haven, Missouri, submitted an overture on evolution to a convention simply asking the convention to urge the praesidium of the LCMS to send a questionnaire to the president and heads of the science departments of all LCMS schools to find out what they are teaching about creation and evolution, the overture was not presented. The LCMS's attorney advised church officials that they could get into legal difficulty if it were published. THIS IS PURE NONSENSE. LCMS officials do not want to open up what some of them know is "a can of worms." They do not want to let the members of the LCMS know that evolution is being promoted in some LCMS schools. It might hurt fund raising efforts.

The LCMS now needs a president who knows something about science and evolution. No candidate for the LCMS presidency has studied evolution and science more and longer than Dr. Kurt Marquart. Among the many candidates for the presidency of the LCMS only Kurt Marquart and Daniel Preus have what it takes to see to it that proper discipline is practiced in the LCMS and that evolutionists like DayStar and Jesus First hero, Matthew Becker, are removed from the LCMS's clergy roster. The LCMS does not need another orthodox but weak conservative president who writes excellent material but allows evolutionists to remain on the LCMS's clergy roster year after year.

When the matter of Genesis and evolution came up during the panel discussion at the Walther Conference, Dr. Marquart noted that if the first Adam is not really historical then faith in second Adam, Jesus Christ, is undermined. Jesus believed Adam was a real person and that Genesis presented historic fact. If Jesus was mistaken than he is not God. If evolution is true and men gradually evolved from some amoebic slime he has gotten better and really needs no Savior from sin. Once the foundation in Genesis is destroyed the whole structure of the Christian faith comes tumbling down. This is what has happened in almost every major denomination.

Note the drawing on p. 9. While many Christians rightly blast away at abortion, divorce, racism, pornography, homosexuality, euthanasia, the Church Growth movement, etc. the humanists with their evolution blast away at the very foundation, Genesis and the Christian doctrine of creation. If the LCMS again elects Dr. Jerry Kieschnick president, evolutionists like Kieschnick supporter Matthew Becker, will continue undermining the very foundation of the Christian faith in the LCMS. The LCMS will continue down the road of "anything goes" churches.

CREATION AND EVOLUTION IN LCMS SCHOOLS

Whereas, At least some of the schools in the Concordia University System appear to be hesitant to take a stand against evolution and for a six day creation; (Note the response to a letter sent to all presidents and

27

chairmen of science departments at schools in the Concordia University System published in the November 4, 2002 Christian News, p. 2); and

Whereas, Dr. Kurt Marquart, a Lutheran Church-Missouri Synod professor, has frequently said that the teaching of evolution as a fact must cease in The Lutheran Church-Missouri schools; therefore be it

Resolved, That the 2004 Convention of The Lutheran Church-Missouri Synod ask the Praesidium of the LCMS to send a similar letter to the presidents and chairmen of the science departments of all LCMS schools in CUS; and be it

Resolved, that the Praesidium publish the results of its survey; and be it

Resolved, that the Praesidium take appropriate action if their survey shows that there are professors at LCMS schools who do not affirm the scriptural position of the LCMS on creation and evolution as confessed in the Brief Statement and the LCMS's 1973 "Statement of Scriptural and Confessional Principles".

Trinity Lutheran Church, New Haven, Missouri

Christian News, February 16, 2004

1. LCMS Professor Matthew Becker denies ____.
2. What is coming in the LCMS? ____.
3. Marquart noted at a Walther Conference that if the Adam is not really historical then ____.
4. Once the foundation in Genesis is destroyed then ____.

DR. KURT MARQUART PRESENTATION
"EVOLUTION IS VOODOO"

By: Allen Spitler, M.D.

Dr. Marquart on April 19, 2004 on the campus of Southeast Missouri State University presented a lecture entitled "Evolution as Voodoo." He then showed a video of International scholars who debated starting from nothing or from an intelligent creator.

Evolution is supported primarily by philosophers and psychologists. Scientist require—at the least—intelligent design. Even Darwin (who's grandfather wrote a book on evolution before his grandson, Charles) espoused a creator of simple organisms—which later 'evolved' to higher forms by the process of selective mutations.

However, we now know mutations ONLY delete genetic information, but DON'T add new information to the genetic pool! Dr. Marquart related a question and answer from a visiting Chinese scientist who presented evidence that refuted the theory of evolution.

When someone in the audience expressed surprise that the Chinese government allowed representatives from China to make such statements, the presenter replied that "In China, one is allowed to talk about evolution, but not the government. In the United States, it seems one can talk about the government, but not evolution". Numerous books and other references were listed in a handout by professor Marquart for anyone interested in delving more deeply into the matter. An admonition was given to separate one's thinking about the Biblical account of creation and the scientific treatment of fossils and methods of dating the age of the earth. His presentation prompted several questions from students and other members of the audience.

Christian News, April 26, 2004

1. Marquart's lecture at Southeast Missouri State University was titled
____.

THE TREES, THE FOREST, AND
PROFESSOR HUBER

By Kurt Marquart

Review of Prof. C. Huber's "Philosophy and the Language of Religion"
(American Lutheran, Jan. 1964.)

Having been favorably impressed with Prof. Curtis Huber's earlier article, "The Language of the Faith" (THE SPRINGFIELDER, Spring, 1962), the present writer accepted with pleasure the assignment to review a more recent article by Prof. Huber, "Philosophy and the Language of Religion," which appeared in the AMERICAN LUTHERAN for January, 1964. The earlier article had revealed a healthy absence of the fashionable anti-intellectualism, and had, despite a weak and needlessly skeptical conclusion, reflected a refreshing independence of judgment. The AMERICAN LUTHERAN piece, however, suggests a point of view which, while still casting longing glances at orthodoxy and freedom, is really already quite imprisoned in the gilded cage of the very theories it seeks to evaluate!

It is always difficult to ride two horses at once, particularly when they are going to opposite directions. And who will try to understand the implications of the two sets of assertions quoted below—if you are not a philosopher, you need look up only "ontological" and "metaphysics"—must realize that they are fundamentally incompatible. Yet both sets occur in the same article:

Set 1

"Science and religion have argued and most of logical necessity argues in vain...It is therefore impossible for the bulk of significant religious claims to function as refutations of scientific claims or to find support in them. The two domains are on different levels because their terms and propositions, in the vital areas we have mentioned, have different meanings...The moral is, of course, to return scientists to their proper work with God's benediction on their labor and remove ourselves from an absurd battlefront to more productive and rationally satisfying effort." (p.9).

Set 2

"This automatically involves us in ontological disputes with the skeptics. And these disputes cannot be settled merely by blaming them on variant preferences for certain ways of talking...Christianity must still address itself to the age-old problems of metaphysics and preserve a wholesome interest in the nature of ultimate reality. The alternative, it seems, is to abandon all interest in truth and meaning" (p. 25).

The article fails to escape obvious self-contradiction only because it consists almost entirely of elaborations on the theme of Set 1. Set 2 is simply chucked in raw, as it were, for good measure. If this latter complex of ideas had been developed instead, then, given the Christian doctrine of Revelation, the article could have been a masterpiece—in which case it would presumably have had to appear in another medium. One gathers that Set 1 represents the author's thinking, and Set 2 his sound religious intuition.

The Fundamental Fallacy

It is impossible to criticize particular statements in the article without first pointing out the fundamental fallacy that underlies the whole presentation, and that is the very idea of "religious language."

Presumably Holy Scripture consists of "religious language." Now, in the Bible we find such diverse types of literature as poetry, narrative, dialogue, historical records, parables, letters, etc., reflecting in turn such diverse realities as commands, promises historical events, quotations, (of true, false, and undecided content), dreams, visions, explanations, etc. In addition there is the multitude of theological books, devotional, doctrinal, exegetical, practical, polemical, orthodox, heterodox, etc. And then there is the welter of pagan religions, with their multifarious mythologies, philosophies, moralities, etc. What possible purpose is served by lumping all these vastly different types of utterance, some true, some false, some literal, some symbolical, some indicative, some imperative, into one category of "religious language," as if they had approximately the same relation to reality? From the standpoint of Christian theology nothing is gained except an invitation to recklessly muddled thinking. The only point of view from which such an improbable classification would make sense is that of naturalism, i.e. anti-theistic unbelief. That view regards observation—as the only reality, and science as the only authentic or "true" description of that reality. Anything beyond this denatured "nature" is unreal, although poets, artists, religionists, and lunatics are encouraged to exercise their "creative imaginations" in this field, particularly if they can help to conjure up some "spiritual values" with which to prevent nuclear war! From this point of view it makes very good sense indeed to banish everything "supernatural" into the limbo of "religious language," where its separation from (scientific) "reality" is *a priori*, methodologically assured. From this limbo only "values" are permitted to ooze out upon "reality," mainly for the benefit of the untutored, unscientific multitudes.

Loss of Over-All Perspective

It would appear then that in accepting the idea of "religious language," Prof. Huber has fallen prey to that nemesis of our age of specialization: a loss of overall perspective through intensive preoccupation with details. He evidently does not see that his theistic, Christian point of view is quite incompatible with the naturalistic, egalitarian concept which must of necessity assign the same validity to all "religious language," whether it deals with the Resurrection of Christ, or with the Buddha's eternal contemplation of his navel. And to expect naturalistic philosophers to arrive at anything but naturalistic conclusions would be the height of folly.

To the Christian theologian it should be abundantly clear that the whole question of the "meaning" of "religious language" is not a genuine problem at all. For Christians it is a pseudo-problem. It was artificially

31

created in an unbelieving attempt to salvage "values" from the *de facto* wreckage of Christianity.

Consider the following statements by one who regards religion as the "ritual cultivation of socially approved values":

"We may regard the tendency to think and behave as if many religious scriptures are literally true, as examples of *verbal* ritual hypertrophy. The belief that the resurrection of Christ was a physical event rather than a symbol of the enduring value of his teachings would be a current example from our own society. I would regard the literal belief in personal immortality as another example, and the list of examples could be extended considerably.

"It is easy to see that what is called here hypertrophy of verbal ritual, or the tendency to behave as if symbolic religious statements and representations are literally true, is one important source of conflict between science and religion.

"If we regard religious dogma as the misinterpretation in literal physical terms of what are primarily value symbols, then this lack of concern with dogma would appear to be a healthy feature in primitive religions, and an excessive concern with dogma would involve an obscuring of the 'real' meaning and force of religion" (John L. Fischer, "The Role of Religion as Viewed by the Science of Man," in *Science Ponders Religion*, ed. By Harlow Shapley, pp. 232, 233, 234-235).

Disbelief in the Whole Thing

Here we have the real problem of "meaning," instead of the pleasant illusions of Prof. Huber and others. It is clear that Prof. Fischer, the author of the foregoing quotes, wishes to find some "meaning" for "religious language." It is equally clear that he is aware of considerable difficulties? Is it that the professor's mind is so imbued with a sense of reality and intellectual honesty that he simply cannot comprehend the intended sense of the assertions of, say, the New Testament? Is it not rather his *disbelief* in the whole thing? Not inability to understand, but unwillingness to believe is the basic and only problem involved. The difficulty is roughly comparable to that of a convinced Christian who would suddenly be compelled to find "meaning" (i.e. validity) in the Thor-cult of Nordic mythology.

No one in his right mind, least of all Christian theologian, will argue that there is any deficiency in the New Testament's *understandability*, which is the only proper meaning of meaning! Why then must we play the silly game of pretending that "understanding" really means "agreeing," when it is obvious that understanding is in fact the indispensable prerequisite for disagreeing? And is the dubious honor of having unbelievers concede "meaning" to some demythologized version of the Faith really worth the trouble of implying the absurdity that a technical treatise on language analysis is more intelligible than the New Testament?

Prof. Huber writes: "Give any statement of the verification principle with its insistence on sense experience as the wellspring of meaning, it is clearly impossible to confirm or falsify statements about a non-temporal, non-spatial, transcendent infinite deity or existence of any kind." Somehow the Christian doctrine of Revelation seems to have been over-looked entirely. Given that doctrine, it is very simple indeed to "confirm or falsify statements" etc.

But what is the relation between statements verified by reference to the authority of empirical observation and rational construction? Are the former less certain than the latter? Or are they simply on "different lev-els?" Neither of these alternatives is tenable.

No Christian theologian worth of the name could agree that Scrip-turally guaranteed assertions are somehow uncertain, while scientific propositions are firm and reliable. For the Christian, truths revealed on the direct authority of God Himself possess absolute certainty and *a priori* take precedence over any assertions made on human authority, no matter how plausible. When Prof. Huber speaks of "the court of scientific respectability" in this connection, he is either engaging in irony, or else he is suffering from an inverted sense of values. In the Christian view of things it is not the bearer of divine revelation, theology, that must come to terms with human science, but vice versa. It is for this reason that genuine theology has never claimed to be "science," in the modern sense of tentative constructs and hypotheses about human observations, al-though theology has always claimed to be "science" in the classical sense of certain knowledge as distinguished from mere opinion.

We must in this connection dispose of some mystical notions which in the name of "imagery" and "paradox" foster an antidogmatic vagueness. That the supernatural mysteries cannot be fathomed by reason, and that they inevitably generate "an irresolvable logical tension...that will forever disturb the carnal mind," is of course sound Christian truth. Chesterton's words apply: "If he saw two truths that seemed to contradict each other, he would take the two truths and the contradiction along with them. His spiritual sight is stereoscopic, like his physical sight: he sees two different pictures at one, yet sees all the better for that" (*Orthodoxy*, London: The Bodley Head, p. 35). We may note in passing that science is forced to do the same thing in its field (viz., "waves" and "particles" in quantum physics). But when Prof. Huber goes on to assert that "we may well have mistaken some of the paradoxical imagery in our confessions and Biblical interpretations (!) for facts of a sort that were never intended," he is on very shaky ground indeed. Why has he not supplied any examples? How does he propose to keep his position from disappearing into neo-orthodox quicksands?

The fact that there are mysteries beyond the ken of reason establishes no presumption against theological exactness and definiteness. Firstly, the fact that the mind can form no clear image of something (e.g. certain complex geometrical figures) does not mean that some, indeed many, pre-cise and definite things may not be affirmed or denied of such objects. Secondly, *stating* a mystery, on the basis of divine revelation is one thing; "*explaining*" it rationally is quite another. The two must not be confused. And unless it were possible state mysteries, how would it be possible to recognize them as mysteries in the first place? (Here the Orthodox Fa-

33

thers, who conveyed mysterious content in rational language, and a decided advantage over the moderns, who confuse everybody by using mysterious language to convey rationalistic content. The advantage was, of course, Revelation). Thirdly, the relevant controversial statements of theology are essentially *negative*. And in order to distinguish an object from other objects, or to say what it is not, it is not necessary to penetrate the mysteries of its interior nature. For example, I may know virtually nothing about New Guinea; yet with the aid of a good map I could both make numerous correct and exact statements about its boundaries, and refute a lot of erroneous ideas on the subject. Fourthly, given a reliable source of information, exact relationships between entities may be known, even if the entities themselves are largely unknown. For example, if I am reliably informed that A. is four years older than B., then this knowledge is valid, exact, etc., even if I haven't the faintest idea of the actual ages of A. and B.

Naturally, all this presupposes that Scripture is a completely reliable, indeed authoritative source of genuine information. Once this elementary assumption of faith is challenged, as in neo-orthodoxy, agnosticism becomes the ruling principle, the only question being what specific form or degree of it best suits one's individual taste. And tragi-heroic poses with a Creed embalmed in skeptical profundities avail nothing, particularly when it is fashionable to pay romantic aspects to the *forms* of the remote past, and to build monuments to the prophets whose theology one rejects!

No "Different Levels"

But are religious and scientific statements perhaps "on different levels?" A study of actual cases and a little reasoning about the nature of the problem should convince anyone of the impossibility of this notion. What is meant by "different levels" anyway? Does this imply that there are two closed systems of reality, each totally unrelated to the other? If not, then what does it mean? Since Christian theology deals not primarily with "a non-temporal, non-spatial, transcendent, infinite deity" but with God Incarnate—with all the earthly, historical particularity which such a view entails—it is clear that many theological statements will necessarily deal also with these aspects of reality which are in principle within the province of scientific inquiry. Does the theory of "levels" imply that science deals with reality on the factual level while theology must content itself with conceding the scientific "level" and merely adding some sort of "creative" or axiological embellishments? If so, the scheme is unacceptable to Christian theology, whose mission it is not to sanction human mythologies, but to confront them with divine reality. But if not, then what *is* meant?

Prof. Huber is quite aware of the positivist short-circuiting of meaning, for he writes that in this scheme "the criterion of meaning (is) itself meaningless on its own showing." But he apparently fails to see the larger implications of the fallacy, and therefore simply accepts the naturalistic equation of the "natural" with the "empirical" or the "scientific."

34

But naturalism, the idea that observable nature is the sum total of reality, is contrary to nature. From such a subnatural point of view, much that is merely natural (e.g. the human soul) appears to be "supernatural," with the unpleasant implication of "unreal."

A Dangerous Half-Truth

Prof. Huber writes: "And because the great religious events of creation, incarnation, salvation, resurrection, conversion and sanctification cannot be explained in terms of natural events which are always open to the scientific method of explanation, they cannot themselves be regarded as natural events." That is a dangerous half-truth. If it is meant to convey the thought that the Incarnation cannot be demonstrated biologically, nor conversion psychologically, then it must be asked; what responsible theologian has ever maintained such or similar lunacy? In this sense, who has ever put "the events of religious importance...in the same category with the natural?" But if the statement means that "religious events" are so independent of "natural events" that the former can co-exist with any version of the latter, then it is patently false. For example, that Joseph was not the biological father of Jesus, or that the tomb of Jesus was empty after the Resurrection, are both assertions involving "natural events." But they are not optional, as if a contradictory account of the "natural events" would do just as well to attack the "religious events" of the Virgin Birth and the Resurrection.

But unless theology surrenders to science, will not the conflict continue? From the Christian standpoint there can be no real conflict between true religion and true science, since the former represents the Creator's own revelation, deposited in Scripture, while the latter is simply systematized observation of the visible creation. So long as both disciplines remain within their proper bounds, no conflict can arise between them.

The Ancient Pagan Evolution Myth

The real conflict is between Christian theism and secularism or naturalism—and that is *philosophy* ("scientism"), not science! The most popular example of a "science-religion conflict" is no doubt the dispute about Evolution. Yet nothing is clearer than that science itself is not a party to the dispute. There may be ever so many scientists who choose a certain world-view in preference to others, but this does not make it scientific. When a scientist dogmatizes and philosophizes the result is not science but—dogmatics and philosophy! And that is exactly what Evolution is. Concerning the scientifically ascertained facts of the case there is no dispute at all between evolutionists and anti-evolutionists. What is debated is the interpretation of the facts, and that obviously depends upon one's general conception of reality. It is then a question of selecting that metaphysical framework which one thinks best suited to the picture presented by the scientific evidence. And the ancient pagan Evolution myth is singularly unsuited to the tested, verified findings of modern science (e.g. the anti-evolutionary fossil record, the explosion of the idea of

35

spontaneous generation, the anti-evolutionary principles of heredity, as established experimentally by modern genetics, etc.)

Is the primitive, evolutionary Nature-cult the sort of thing to which we ought to "return scientists...with God's benediction?" Hardly. But if this is not what is meant, then where on earth is that "absurd battlefront" to be found, from which we must "remove ourselves?" And, as has already been shown, nothing is gained by talking about "different levels." It is manifestly absurd to assert that Evolution is true at one level, but not at another. Either it happened or it did not happen. Either Scripture or scientism teaches a myth concerning the origin of man. "Reconciling" the conflict by talking about "different levels" is a polite way of declaring the Bible irrelevant to the whole realm of fact, and allowing it to function only "emotively," like Aesop's Fables. It is this sort of cheap apologetics which invites quips like H.G. Wells' about the (Anglican) Bishops, who, "socially so much in evidence, are intellectually in hiding."

One final comment concerns Prof. Huber's statements about the "emotive-conative capability" of language, and his recommendation of an understanding of the "power of all language" as an antidote to "the coldness of traditional orthodoxy and the impotence of its rationalistic appeal." This comes dangerously close to substituting a "power of words" for the power of the Word, I Cor. 2:4. And it is worth pondering the curious paradox that the eloquent sermons of gifted, learned men often seem to produce a kind of dilettante religiosity while the plain, artless, "humdrum," even clumsy preaching of simple men of God produces striking examples of rugged faith! As for the "coldness" and "rationalistic appeal" of "traditional orthodoxy," they are simply ill-informed inventions. It is significant that the Old Lutherans who were hounded out of Europe in the last century were accused by their Rationalistic opponents of being "mystics!" If Prof. Huber finds contemporary Lutheran preaching "cold" and "rationalistic," the fault lies not with "traditional orthodoxy," but with the various un-Lutheran influences which are supposed to be "enriching" it, e.g. pietism, moralism, Reformed anti-sacramentalism, Rationalism, doctrinal confusion and indifference, not to mention the deadening forces of conformism and organizationalism ("stewardship"!) and the increasing secularization—largely via the seminaries—of the Ministerial Office, with the attendant destruction of a sense of vocation and of spiritual direction among the clergy.

The over-all lesson to be learned from Prof. Huber's article is the melancholy but obvious one that the attempt to solve theological problems by means of "implications" imported from naturalistic philosophy, is a wretchedly unproductive and futile enterprise. One can only hope that the authorities at the Springfield Seminary will see to it that its students are directed "to more productive and rationally satisfying effort"!

K. Marquart

Christian News, March 23, 1964

Editor's Note: When Christian News sent Dr. Curtis Huber Marquart's article for comment or refutation, he replied with a post card: "Mr. Otten, Drop Dead. C. E. Huber."

1. It is difficult to ride two horses at once when they are ____.
2. Where did Prof. Huber's "Philosophy and the Language of Religion" appear? ____.
3. From the Christian standpoint there can be no real conflict between true ____ and true ____.
4. The ancient pagan evolution myth is unsuited to be tested, verified findings of modern ____.
5. What is a wretchedly unproductive and futile enterprise? ____.

CHRISTIANITY AND FREEMASONRY

I. Preliminary Observation: Can Outsiders Know Masonic Teachings?

Many people have the Impression that an outsider cannot possibly discuss the Craft with a Mason, because the former can have no knowledge of the Craft which could be proved correct, while the latter is bound to absolute silence.

It will therefore come as a surprise to many, to learn that according to the HIGHEST MASONIC AUTHORITY ANYONE may know the religious philosophy of Freemasonry, since only the rituals, modes of recognition, etc., are secret, but not "the Masonic Creed."

The following statements are taken from the latest edition (seventh printing, 1956) of Albert Mackey's ENCYCLOPEDIA OF FREEMASONRY (Revised), published as "The World's Greatest Masonic Authority" by The Masonic History Company, 2300 S. Michigan Avenue, Chicago, Illinois, U.S.A., and obtainable from there by anyone for 25 dollars. In the front of the book there appears the note: "IMPORTANT. Standard and fully approved works on the subject of Freemasonry are published only by The Masonic History Company."

Under "Secret Doctrine," (vol. R, p. 920) the ENCYCLOPEDIA says:

All mystical societies, and even liberal philosophers, were to a comparatively recent period accustomed to veil the true meaning of their instructions in intentional obscurity, lest the unlearned and uninitiated should be offended. The Ancient Mysteries had their secret doctrine; so had the school of Pythagoras, and the sect of the Gnostics . . . FREEMASONRY ALONE HAS NO SECRET DOCTRINE. ITS PHILOSOPHY IS OPEN TO THE WORLD. Its modes of recognition by which it secures identification, and its rites and ceremonies which are its method of instruction, alone are secret. ALL MEN MAY KNOW THE TENETS OF THE MASONIC CREED.

And again, under "Secret Societies," (VOL II, p. 922):

. . . Freemasonry . . . is a secret society only as respects its signs, a few of its legends and traditions, and its method of inculcating its mystical philosophy, but which, as to everything else—its design, its object, its moral and RELIGIOUS TENETS, AND THE GREAT DOCTRINE WHICH IT TEACHES—IS AS OPEN A SOCIETY AS IF IT MET ON THE HIGHWAYS BENEATH THE SUN OF DAY, AND NOT WITHIN THE WELL-GUARDED PORTALS OF A LODGE. (our emphases)

So the Masonic Creed is quite open to public discussion— and that is really the most vital aspect. But even the rituals and other matters can be discovered by anyone without too much trouble. In the first place, most of these "secrets" are printed in official Masonic publications, either quite openly or else in an easily decipherable code. In the second place, many former Masons have written books about the Craft, so that there is really no doubt whatever as to what goes on in the Lodge. And it should not be forgotten that those who leave the Lodge for conscience's sake, usually turn over all the authentic information they possess to their pastors!

We can be done then with the argument that Masonry cannot be discussed, fully confident that all the necessary authentic evidence is available.

II. Preliminary Observation: Defining the Issue.

It is not correct to say that the Church is "against Masons." The Church isn't against any individual. But precisely because she is profoundly and compassionately FOR each human being, she is AGAINST all systems, opinions, and teachings which, from the divine Revelation in Scripture she knows to be harmful and wrong. The argument has nothing to do with anyone's personal sincerity or character. It should be viewed strictly objectively: Are there objective conflicts between the teachings of Christianity and those of Masonry? It is the argument of this article that Masonry and Christianity are two mutually exclusive, incompatible religious systems, and that no human being can CONSISTENTLY be both a Christian and a Mason. That many Christians appear to find no conflict, we grant. But such people misunderstand either Christianity or Masonry, or both. It is the argument and position of the Church that no one who knows both what Christianity is and what Masonry is, can be both a Christian and a Mason. Anyone who is or seems to be both, is not true to one of his mutually exclusive loyalties.

This should also make it plain to anyone that the Church's objection is not mere traditionalism, or temporary "cultural lag," but is as permanent and as incorrigible, as the Christian Faith itself.

We repeat, that all this should not be construed as a personal judgment on any individual. The argument is based on official documents.

III. First Basic Conflict: Christianity and Masonry have a different God.

A. Masonry Is a Religion.

This is usually denied. But how can it NOT be a religion, when it has temples, altars, doctrines, worship, chaplains, etc.? Mackey's ENCYCLOPEDIA settles the question:

> There has been a needless expenditure of ingenuity and talent by a large number of Masonic orators and essayists, in the endeavor to prove that Freemasonry is not a religion . . . Freemasonry is . . . an eminently religious institution. . . Freemasonry may rightfully claim to be called a religious institution. (Vol R, p. 847 "Religion of Freemasonry").

B. Masonic Religion Tries to Include All Religions and Gods.

Mackey: (vol. II, pp 847 ff):

> Freemasonry is not Christianity, nor a substitute for it . . . But the

39

religion of Freemasonry is not sectarian. It admits men of every creed within its hospitable bosom, rejecting none and approving none for his peculiar faith . . .Its religion is that general one of nature and primitive revelation—handed down to us from some ancient and Patriarchal Priesthood—in which all men may agree and no man can differ.

R. Swinburne Clymer, ANCIENT MYSTIC ORIENTAL MASONRY: Masonry is the universal religion only because and only so long as it embraces all religions. . . Masonry is not only a universal science, but a WORLD-WIDE RELIGION, and owes allegiance to no one creed, and can adopt no sectarian dogma, without ceasing thereby to be Masonic. . . Without any references to forms and modes of faith, it furnishes a series of indirect evidences which silently operate to establish the great and general principles of religion, and points to that triumphant system which was the object of all preceding dispensations, and must ultimately be the sole RELIGION OF THE HUMAN RACE." (pp 58-118 Our emphases)

C. Christianity conflicts with Masonic Universalism:

Exodus 20:3: Thou shalt have no other gods before Me!

St. John 5:23: All men should honor the Son even as they honor the Father. He that honoreth not the Son, honoreth not the Father, which hath sent Him.

St. John 14:6: "I am the Way, the Truth, and the Life: no man cometh unto the Father but by Me."

Romans 16:17: Mark them which cause divisions and offenses contrary to the doctrine which ye have learned; and avoid them.

II Cor . 6:13 ff.: Be ye not unequally yoked together with unbelievers . . . Wherefore come out from among them, and be ye separate, saith the Lord.

Galatians l:8ff: But though we, or an angel from heaven, preach any other gospel unto you than that which we have preached unto you, let him be accursed.

I John 2:22ff: Who is a liar but he that denieth that Jesus is the Christ? He is antichrist, that denieth the Father and the Son. Whosoever denieth the Son, the same hath not the Father.

II John 9 ff: Whosoever transgresseth, and abideth not in the doctrine of Christ, hath not God. He that abideth in the doctrine of Christ, he hath both the Father and the Son. If there come any unto you, and bring not this doctrine, receive him not into your house, neither bid him God speed: For he that biddeth him God speed is partaker of his evil deeds.

D. Objection: Masonry Uses the Christian Bible and Therefore Cannot Be Anti-Christian.

Reply: Masonry does not use the Bible as divine truth, but only as a symbol of divine truth, on the same level with the Koran and other pagan books. Proof:

Mackey, Volume I, p. 133 ("Bible"):

The Bible is properly called a greater light of Freemasonry, for from the center of the Lodge it pours forth upon the East, the West, and the South its refulgent rays of Divine truth. The Bible is used among Freemasons as a symbol of the will of God, however it may be expressed. Therefore, whatever to any people expresses that well may be used as a substitute for the Bible in a Masonic Lodge. Thus, in a Lodge consisting entirely of Jews, the Old Testament alone may be placed upon the altar, and Turkish Freemasons make use of the Koran. Whether it be the Gospels to the Christian, the Pentateuch to the Israelite, the Koran to the Mussulman, or the Vedas to the Brahman, it everywhere Masonically conveys the same idea—that of the symbolism of the Divine Will revealed to man.

From the introduction to a Masonic edition of the Bible, written by H.L. Haywood, "Masonry's greatest living writer and scholar,":

The Bible itself has a similar multiplicity of uses and meanings; it is the Bible and at the same time is the volume of the Sacred Law; it is the Book of the Old and New Testaments and at the same time represents each of the world Bibles, and may *be* replaced by the Koran, the Zend Avesta, the Vedas, etc.; it lies on the Altar and yet does not have possession of it because the Square and Compasses lie on the Altar with it; . . . the Lodge uses it as the LITERATURE of religion; . . . Masons . . , employ it for purposes of their own and apply to it definitions peculiar to themselves.

III. Second Basic Conflict: Christianity and Masonry Teach Different Roads to Salvation.

The basic moral doctrine of Masonry is that man is "saved" not by the merit of Christ, but by his own merit, effort, morality, character, etc. Masonry uses geometrical allegory to teach this system of self-salvation.

Mackey (Volume I, p. 499), under "Jacob's Ladder," a Masonic symbol:

Its three principal rounds, representing Faith, Hope, and Charity, present us with the means of advancing from earth to heaven, from death to life—from the mortal to immortality. Hence its foot is placed on the ground floor of the Lodge, which is typical of the world, and its top rests on the covering of the Lodge, which is symbolic of heaven.

That "Faith" here cannot be understood in the Christian sense of trust in the Redemption of Christ, is clear from the fact that Masonry is open not only to Christians, but also to Jews, Mohammodans, etc.

The Lamb-skin given to the Mason upon his initiation is to be:

an ever-present reminder of that "purity of heart and uprightness of conduct so essentially necessary," thus keeping pure your thoughts, and inspiring nobler deeds and greater achievements! (Masonic Ritual of the State of Texas, U.S.A., p. 208)

The lamb-skin is given to Christian and non-Christian alike, making it clear that Masonry offers a way of salvation which has nothing to do with Christ's Redemption. The Lamb-skin lecture concludes:

. . . may the record of your life and actions be as pure and spotless

41

as this Apron now is; and when your soul, freed from earth, shall stand naked and alone before the Great White Throne, may it be your portion to hear from Him Who sits thereon, the welcome plaudit: "Well done, thou good and faithful servant! Enter thou into the joy of thy Lord!"

Clymer, ANCIENT MYSTIC ORIENTAL MASONRY:

Every soul must "Work out his own salvation." Salvation by faith and the vicarious atonement were not taught, as now interpreted, by Jesus . . . Masonry does not teach salvation by faith, nor the Vicarious Atonement. Go through its degrees, study the history as taught by its greatest Masters, and you cannot find that it teaches this doctrine. Boldly do I claim that this doctrine does not make Christians, but it does make criminals. (pp. 10-11)

Now compare all this with the doctrine of the Sacred Scriptures:

St. John 3:36: He that believeth on the Son hath everlasting life: and he that believeth not the Son shall not see life; but the wrath of God abideth on him.

St. John 14:6: I am the way, the truth, and the life, no man cometh unto the Father but by Me.

Acts 4:12: Neither is there salvation in any other: for there is none other name under heaven given among men, whereby we must be saved.

Galatians 3:11: No man is justified by the Law in the sight of God.

Ephesians 2:8 ff: For by grace are ye saved through faith; and that not of yourselves: it is the gift of God: Not of works, lest any man should boast.

I John 5:12: He that hath the Son hath life; and he that hath not the Son of God hath not life.

IV. The Conflict Is Admitted Not Only From the Christian, But Also From the Masonic Side:

Not only Roman Catholics, Eastern Orthodox, and Lutherans have condemned the religious teachings of Freemasonry (and these three churches alone constitute an overwhelming majority of Christians), but the conservative Reformed or Calvinistic bodies too have rejected Masonry, for example, conservative Presbyterians, Reformed, Methodists, and Baptists. In fact, as Fr. Hannah points out in DARKNESS VISIBLE:

NO CHURCH THAT HAS SERIOUSLY INVESTIGATED THE RELIGIOUS TEACHINGS AND IMPLICATIONS OF FREEMASONRY HAS EVER YET FAILED TO CONDEMN IT. (p. 78)

"The Relation of the Liberal Churches and the Fraternal Orders" is a pamphlet by Elijah Alfred Coil, a Master Mason, and a Unitarian minister (Unitarianism denies the Blessed Trinity, the Divinity of Christ, and consequently, the Redemption). The following statements appear in this pamphlet (pp. 10-15):

Nearly all of those monitors have, as their very heart, the fatherhood of God, the brotherhood of man, immortality, and salvation by character, principles very familiar to every Unitarian Sunday

42

School scholar who has been properly taught the fundamentals of our faith.

That the fundamental difference in the principles embodied in the historic creeds of Christendom and those of our modern secret orders has not been clearly thought out is indicated by the fact that many pledge themselves to both. There are lodge men who, in the churches, subscribe to the doctrine that "We are accounted righteous before God only for the merit of our Lord and Savior Jesus Christ, by faith and not for our own works or deservings," and enthusiastically join in the singing of hymns in which that idea is embodied. Then in their lodge meetings they just as enthusiastically assent to the following declaration: "Although our thoughts, words and actions may be hidden from the eyes of men, yet that All-Seeing Eye whom the sun, moon and stars obey, and under whose watchful care even comets perform their stupendous revolutions, pervades the inmost recesses of the human heart, and will reward us according to our merits." A little child, once its attention is called to the matter, ought to be able to see that it is impossible to harmonize the creed statement here quoted, with the declaration taken from the monitor of one of our greatest and most effective secret orders, and found, in substance, in the liturgies of nearly all the others. If "We are accounted righteous before God only for the merit of our Lord and Savior, Jesus Christ, by faith and not for our own works or deservings," then it cannot possibly be true that the All Seeing Eye "Pervades the inmost recesses of the human heart, and will reward us according to our merits." One of these declarations excludes the other. Men cannot consistently subscribe to both.

Fraternity men, interested in the welfare of their children, should be informed that in the liberal churches (modernist and Unitarian, K.M.) their children will be trained in principles which they will now practically have to deny, should they become members of the lodge.

And Mr. Coil argues, quite consistently, that Masons should leave their conservative Christians church-bodies, and unite with those which deny the historic Christian Faith!

In reply to the Church of England's Fr. W. Hannah's book DARKNESS VISIBLE, there appeared, anonymously, LIGHT INVISIBLE, by one who is both a Mason and a Church of England minister. The dust jacket speaks of the author's "profound Masonic knowledge and insight," and styles the book "a clear, logical, and irrefutable answer." An editorial review of the book in FREEMASONS MAGAZINE, No. 677 (published from Great Queen Street, London, and styled "The Organ of the Craft,") praises this book as an "authoritative" statement of Masonic principles. Excerpts follow:

... were Mr , Hannah's excessively exclusive and narrow interpretation of Christianity the true one, it would indeed be incompatible with the broader spirit of Freemasonry which sees truth in all religions and gives precedence to none in its religious observances,

(p. 42)

How then does Mr. Hannah profess to build up a case against our ancient and honorable fraternity? He does so only by presenting a distorted and un-Christian interpretation of Christianity. He neither knows nor cares to know anything of comparative religion. Christianity, he says again and again, is an exclusive faith. Christ opened the only gate of heaven to man below. All prayer not offered in the name of Christ, he boldly proclaims, is idolatrous. He is our only mediator and advocate, and the only revelation of divine truth. In His name only is salvation to be found.

If Mr. Hannah is right, he has certainly proved his case. Given these premises, his logic is undoubtedly irrefutable. If true religion is thus to be narrowed down to salvation in no other name under heaven, and St. Paul's (should be St. Peter's, Acts 4:12, K.M.) words to this effect be understood in a spirit of bigoted literalness, then any such "Christian" must indeed lie straining his conscience to the breaking point by accepting initiation into the broader and deeper mysteries of Freemasonry. I for one can never understand how anyone who takes an exclusive view of Christ as the only complete revelation of God's truth can become a Freemason without suffering from spiritual schizophrenia . . . the really honest Mason who is capable of logical reasoning must realize that such a dual allegiance is difficult to reconcile with spiritual integrity. If that is conceding a point to Mr. Hannah, he is welcome to it. (That isn't just "a point" that's the whole case, K.M.) . . .

If it is wrong for a Christian to pray together with the Jew or Moslem to the Great Architect, then it is undoubtedly wrong for him to become a Mason, (pp. 48-49).

For, if a Christian and a Hindu meet together in a Lodge, and pray together to God, it is surely axiomatic in this atmosphere of broad charity that the CHRISTIAN MUST ACKNOWLEDGE THAT THE HINDU'S GOD IS ULTIMATELY THE SAME AS HIS OWN, for the prayers in the Masonic Ritual are not of course offered in the plural as to many Gods, but to one. Masonry is monotheistic though wide differences in interpretation of God are of course allowed. It is important that all critics of Masonry as well as Masons themselves, should thoroughly grasp this point.

Is such an attitude incompatible with Christianity? Again, if it is, without doubt Masonry stands condemned, (p. 59).

The liberal Christian has more in common with the liberal Jew or the liberal Buddhist than he has with the bigotries of either extreme Protestantism or extreme Catholicism, Anglo or Roman, (p. 61).

In this book I have tried above all things to be completely honest and open. Frankness and candor can hurt no one, and many Masons with previous defenses of the Craft against former attacks have sometimes tended to lack candor through being written in the idiom of the attacker. That is, the religious side of Freemasonry has all

44

too often been played down to the level of the knife-and-fork Masons' conception of it, in the language and phraseology of Christian theology, in order to pacify a narrow and exclusive interpretation of Christianity which can brook no rival. In other words, Freemasonry has been defended on premises and arguments which the loyal honest Mason cannot altogether wholeheartedly accept. (pp. 13-14).

V. Further Points of Conflict: Oaths, Fellowship.

In order to emphasize the major issues, we have not detailed other, subsidiary objections, which, however, should at least be mentioned.

The dreadful oaths of Masonry are immoral from the Christian point of view not only because of the macabre punishments invoked ("your throat cut across, your tongue torn out by the root," etc.) in the Name of God, but also because it is sinful to swear in UNCERTAIN matters. For the oaths are required BEFORE the candidate discovers the "secrets."

Either the oaths are taken seriously, but then they are blasphemous (cursing and swearing by God's Name). Or else they are not taken seriously, but then they are also blasphemous (literally taking the Name of the Lord in vain)! This reflects the general dilemma of Freemasonry: Either it is taken seriously, but then it is a sin against the First Commandment (Idolatry), or else it is not taken seriously, but then it is a sin against the Second Commandment (Blasphemy, taking the Name of the Lord in vain).

Another issue has to do with the unity of the Church. How can a Christian segregate himself from his fellow-Christians, and unite with non-Christians in a religious fraternity, in the face of such clear divine commands as II Cor. 6:13 ff.? What sort of superficial views of the Church and its unity and fellowship does this presuppose? The Church then is reduced to the level of one club among others! And what becomes of the pastoral relation? A Christian must be able to discuss his spiritual life freely with his pastor, who is his confessor. But the Mason cannot go to his non-Masonic pastor to discuss the Masonic part of his religious life! Such a situation is intolerable, to anyone who takes seriously the doctrines of the Church and of the Office of the Keys.

VI. Concluding Observations

Persons interested in further study of this subject are advised to obtain some of the literature here referred to. In this article our object has been merely to show to the satisfaction of any fair, unprejudiced person that the religious system of Freemasonry and the historic Christian religion are totally incompatible, and that no man can therefore CONSISTENTLY be both a Christian and a Mason. We have not argued here the TRUTH of the Church's Faith, but merely its LOGIC in relation to Freemasonry.

The reader, whether Christian or Mason, or both, is asked to weigh the matter carefully, conscientiously, and prayerfully, for nothing less than eternal salvation is at stake! Let no one be confused by false, irrelevant arguments, which have nothing whatever to do with the case. For example: (1) "Many good people belong to the Lodge." True, but our authority in religion are not "good people," but the Bible. The best people can be mistaken. (2) "Clergy belong to the Craft." Yes, unfortunately! But clergy also crucified Christ! (3) "The Craft does welfare work." Yes, but so do other religions. That doesn't make them true!

Each individual will, in the privacy of his own conscience as well as in his outward affiliations, have to make his choice between Christ's Redemption and Masonic self-salvation, the Most Holy Trinity and the "Great Architect of the Universe," the Church and the Craft. Where do you stand:

Here?:
". . . in the confession of the ONLY TRUE GOD we worship the Trinity in Person and the Unity in Substance, of Majesty co-equal" (Communion Preface)

Or

Here?:
"Father of all! In every age, in every clime adored, by saint, by savage, and by sage, Jehovah, Jove, or Lord!" (The UNIVERSAL PRAYER, oft quoted in Masonic instruction," ENCYCLOPEDIA, VOL. II, p. 791)

Christian News, March 18,1968

1. Is the Masonic creed open to public discussion? ____.
2. Is the Church "against Masons?" ____.
3. The Church is against all ____.
4. No one can both consistently be both a ____ and a ____.
5. Mackey's Encyclopedia says that Masonry is a ____.
6. Christianity conflicts with Masonic ____.
7. Christianity and Masonry teach different roads to ____.
8. Unitarianism denies ____.
9. The oaths of Masonry are ____.
10. What is the difference between Masonry and Christianity? ____.

"PROFUMIGATION?"

The rude shock administered to the British Government by the Profumo affair—so luridly dwelt upon by the press—suggests at least three applications to the present ecclesiastical struggles:

I.

Administrations, particularly somewhat senile and tremulous ones, prefer comforting illusions to distressing realities. There is no will to understand the real import of factual evidence. Instead, such evidence is explained away as optimistically as possible! Mr. Macmillan, it transpired, had been warned. But he chose naively to accept rather flimsy explanations. Result! The muddling required to avoid a relatively minor scandal, one, moreover, in which public opinion could have been enlisted on the side of the Government, directly produced a major scandal with disastrous implications. "He who sits on lid of steam-kettle, will have blow up." If Confucius didn't say that, he should have.

The parallel is obvious. Responsible Missouri Synod officials have been warned years ago about the scandalous involvements of leading theologians with heresy. But in the interests of avoiding the unpleasantness which would have resulted from courageous action, the Administration chose to accept childish and flimsy "explanations." Has this bankrupt policy prevented explosions, or reduced them? On the contrary! The Missouri "Government" has reeled from one crisis to the next, and the denotations are getting stronger, not weaker! The last state of that Synod is worse than the first. He that will save his life, shall lose it!

It is safe to assume that had Missouri Synod officials (or Mr. Macmillan, for that matter) for seen the end result of their cover-ups, they would have taken the bull by the horns at the very outset. Had the members of the Praesidium foreseen the indignities which a Scharlemann*, say, finally managed to inflict upon them and the Missouri Synod, they might have refused to be a party to them. But this kind of foresight is not granted to a policy of deliberate alienation from reality and unwillingness to cope with it. He who will not see, finally cannot see. And so the Administration throughout the drawn-out Scharlemann affair, for example, gave the impression of being led along from one surprise to the next in the old "salami" system of attrition: No individual slice is considered worth fighting for, until only the string remains; and then that isn't worth fighting for either! Occasionally one heard rumors that "this time" the officials were really going to take Scharlemann in hand. But the bark soon subsided and no bite ensued. A new white-wash again claimed to have settled everything—until the inevitable next time!

II.

The evidence which produced the Profumo blow-up was insignificant compared to the evidence which should cause a Missouri blow-up, but doesn't—at least so far as the Administration is concerned. After all, there is no evidence at all, that Miss Keeler actually got State secrets out of Mr. Profumo, for her Russian boy-friend(s). The mere possibility was shocking enough.

In the Missouri Synod, however, infection with heresy is not a mere possibility, but an accomplished, documented fact. At least Mr. Profumo was sacked immediately, when his conduct became a matter of public record. Missouri theologians, however, are allowed, year after year, to go on record publicly as being in league with the Enemy (Rationalism, Neo-Orthodoxy), and all that results is chatter, i. e. "statements," "interpretations," "explanations," "discussions," etc, etc. *usque ad nauseam.* Try to imagine Mr. Macmillan keeping a Cabinet Minister on for years and years, for the purpose of instructing him in the virtues of parliamentary democracy, if that gentleman were publicly known to be also, say, a professor of political science at Peiping University, or an associate editor of *Pravda*, in charge of a special column instructing agents in the art of "constructive subversion, encirclement, and infiltration!" (And imagine the guffaws in the Kremlin, were Mr. Macmillan to defend the situation thus: "The Minister will attempt to change *Pravda* for the better!") Such prospects, with respect to the British Government, exist of course only in the world of caricatures and cartoons.

In the Missouri Synod, however, they are the melancholy reality! Do even rather decadent State Administrations nowadays excel Church Administrations in integrity? Have we lost faith in the Day of Judgment?

III.

There is, however, a basic advantage which ecclesiastical "governments" have, that poor Mr. Macmillan did not: the knout of "charity," with which to keep things quiet. As taught by Our Lord, and His holy Apostles, Charity is a divine; principled selflessness, peculiarly unsuited to the role of defender of vested organizational interests. Truth and love divide (Matthew 10:34 ff), as well as unite! And "Charity rejoiceth not in iniquity, but rejoiceth in the truth" 1 Corinthians 13:6.

Like Communism, modern ecclesiasticism has adopted an Orwellian "newspeak," in which many words mean the opposite of what they used to mean. "Love" is a case in point. It would be bad enough if it were defined simply in the sense of an idolatrous humanitarianism: "Thou shalt love thy neighbor with all thy heart, and with all thy soul, and with all thy mind." But when absolute moral norms and limitations are gone, this undifferentiated "love" soon degenerates into an intolerable collectivistic oppression, presided over by "Big Brother." The Group or the Organization now becomes god, and love is defined with reference to it. Whatever advances the Organization is in harmony with Love. Whatever disturbs the Organization is an act of Hate. "Love" now is the sticky, oleaginous goo, required to lubricate the Machinery, and to keep it running smoothly!

From this vantage-point, all the seeming contradictions and hypocrisies of institutionalized Love, which so disturb traditional, unso-

48

phisticated consciences, make "good" sense: If anyone teaches heretical notions, that is not in itself contrary to Love. But if it becomes an Organizational disturbance, then IN THAT SENSE it is a sin and must be apologized for (but the heresy need not be retracted) to Synod, in Convention assembled, which then, in its function as Supreme Custodian and Dispenser of Love, must pronounce its absolution. The real enemy, however, is not he who teaches false doctrine (what's that, anyway?) but he who protests against it. For if it were not for such Apostles of Hate, no disturbance would be caused by heresy, and the Organization could function normally. Hence, when Confessional men attack, criticize, and expose errorists and their patrons, this is Hate, for it disrupts the Organization. But when Organization Men meet every criticism, every assertion of Truth, not by examining the evidence, but by maligning, slandering, smearing, threatening, black-listing, suspending, expelling, and generally persecuting the Confessional men, this is the purest Love! Such is the real nature of that ugly, legalistic, ruthless opportunism, which, amid shrill propaganda about Love and Evangelical Procedure, captures would-be "up-to date" church bodies, when they temporize with objective, revealed Truth. "Love" which throws Truth to the winds, has denied itself! Secular politicians at least cannot call suppression "Love."

Editor's note: Dr. Martin Scharlemann later repudiated the position on the Bible he defended in several of his essays. He was a signer of "Crossroads" (Christian News, January 22, 1973), a statement which endorsed "A Statement on Confessional Principles" adopted at the LCMS's 1973 convention. This statement affirmed the inerrancy of the Bible in all matters and confessed that Christianity is the only saving faith. The December 22, 1979 Christian News published a letter Scharlemann sent to Newsweek defending the position of the LCMS after Newsweek had disguised falsehood as truth. Scharlemann helped Christian News with various revisions of An American Translation of the Bible. He withdrew the charges he had made vs. the CN editor and Kurt Marquart.

Lutheran News, July 29, 1963

1. Administrations, particularly somewhat senile and tremulous ones, prefer comforting illusions to ____.
2. What was the Profumo affair which rocked the British government? ____.
3. Heresy in the LCMS was a ____.
4. What had the LCMS administration done about heresy? ____.
5. How was "love" being misused in the Missouri Synod? ____.

FROM LUTHER TO KIERKEGAARD

FROM LUTHER TO KIERKEGAARD. By Concordia Publishing House, St. Louis, 1963. Paperback.

Concordia Publishing House has announced in the October 1, 1963 *Lutheran Witness* that it just reprinted Dr. Jaroslav Pelikan's *From Luther To Kierkegaard*. Dr. Pelikan began this study in the history of theology while a member of the Department of Philosophy at Valparaiso University and completed it while a member of the Department of Systematic Theology at Concordia Seminary, St. Louis. Concordia first published *From Luther to Kierkegaard* in 1950. Although he is still a member of the Lutheran Church-Missouri Synod, Dr. Pelikan is now Titus Street Professor of Ecclesiastical History at the Divinity School of Yale University. He is the coeditor of the 56-volume *Luther's Works* series, American Edition, currently being published by Concordia Publishing House and Fortress Press.

From Luther to Kierkegaard is divided into five chapters, the titles of which reflect the natural chronological progression of Dr. Pelikan's subject-matter: (1) Luther; (2) Melanchthon and the Confessional Generation; (3) The Age of Orthodoxy; (4) Rationalism; (5) The Nineteenth Century.

The doctrinal history of the Lutheran Church from Luther to the present, along with the philosophical implications involved in this history, Dr. Pelikan briefly summarizes as follows:

Luther had a powerful experience of the Christian Gospel, which caused him to break the bonds of the established Aristotelian-Thomistic tradition. Being a spiritually virile Christian, he was not inclined to be a systematician. His friend Melanchthon took over the task of systematization. Being a confirmed Aristotelian, Melanchthon really corrupted Luther's "existential", personal, vital, etc. theology, and substituted for it a placid, philosophical intellectualism.

For Luther's *fiducia cordis* he substituted intellectual assent to certain propositions. This Protestant scholasticism was ultimately challenged on the basis of its production of monstrous excrescences like the application of the substance-and-accidents categories to hamartiology (p. 47). Finally theological Melanchthonianism was defeated and rejected in the Formula of Concord. But its twin evil, i.e. philosophical Melanchthonianism, Lutheran Aristotelianism, or Protestant scholasticism, to name only a few of the choice epithets which Pelikan chooses to apply to post-Luther Lutheran "philosophy", was embodied in the Confessions themselves, and was in fact rescued for subsequent Lutheranism by Martin Chemnitz, whom Dr. Walther had the misfortune to call "the instrument that God selected for the reconstruction of an almost ruined Lutheran Church" (p. 43). Thereafter Lutheran Orthodoxy developed from this given embryo. Orthodoxy prepared the ground for Rationalism by making the Christian faith and theology a matter of verbal propositions drawn from a mechanically inerrant Bible. This intellectualism of course obscured the very essence of Christianity. Rationalism took up the challenge of Orthodoxy, and found its dogmata wanting on rational grounds. Kant came along and destroyed the epistemological presuppositions of both Orthodoxy and Rationalism. To fill the vacuum he supplied, in his *Critique of Practical Reason*, his famous "categorical imperative", i.e. moralism. Schleiermacher, in despair over the collapse of confidence in man's mind, and in opposition to Kant's foundation of religion and on the will, based his "theology" on the third member of the trichotomy, i.e. the feeling, thus founding aestheticism. Kierkegaard finally came upon the scene and recovered Luther's long-lost "existential" emphases. Presently Lutheranism as yet has no philosophy. The philosophy of Orthodoxy has become impossible, and something ought to be done to solve the problem created by the lack of a philosophy, which, after all is necessary for any theology. A solution of the problem should be informed by the insights of Kierkegaard.

This appears to be the essence of Pelikan's message. It might well have been entitled, "The Deformation of the Lutheran Church," for if the book is right, Lutheranism is indeed in a bad state of affairs. With all due respect to Dr. Pelikan's celebrated learning, a "traditional" Lutheran cannot but be irrevocably and entirely opposed to his by no means original theory, the publication of which by Concordia Publishing House (!) is startling demonstration of the alarming extent to which theological discrimination has disappeared from the Missouri Synod. This reviewer rejects categorically the thesis of a learned and well-known theologian for the following reasons:

Secondary Sources

(1) *From Luther to Kierkegaard* appears to be a series of generalizations, based mostly on secondary sources, and moving along confidently at a stratospheric level of abstraction, without thorough documentation from primary sources. Compared with the painstakingly documented *The Inspiration of Scripture* by Dr. Robert Preus, for instance, the present volume appears unconvincing flashy, superficial and considering the scope and importance of the subject, even presumptuous. After all, when a young man finds it necessary to oppose himself and his theories, in such a basic matter, to the continuous and unanimous tradition of centuries of orthodox Lutheranism, with the implication that generations of pious and honored doctors of the Church were basically wrong, while he is right, one would expect to find something more than a flighty and sketchy treatise obscured by the substitution of vague, evasive formulations and insinuations for direct and explicit statements at crucial points, and supported almost entirely by secondary sources, at least in important conclusions.

Much of the book becomes painfully predictable when one reads in the author's preface that he has been influenced by the work "of Karl Holl, the latter through Wilhelm Pauck, who was Holl's pupil and, in turn, my teacher." (p. VI). The position of the book becomes explicable when one sees with what deference the Lundesian school (largely influenced by Holl) and such theologians as Brunner are treated. Tell me who your friends are, and I'll tell you who you are...

Misrepresentation

(2)The interrelations between Luther, Melanchthon, and Aristotle are portrayed so selectively as to warrant the charge of misrepresentation. In a section entitled, "Luther's Ambivalence Toward Philosophy," Dr. Pelikan states that Luther "forbids the study of Aristotle's *Physica* in the schools while endorsing the reading of the *Poetica*" (p. 11). A point is made of the fact that Luther calls Aristotle a "damned pagan", and the general implication of the whole section is that Luther had little or no use for Aristotle. But what are the facts of the case? In his *An den christlichen Adel deutscher Nation* (St. Louis Edition, vol. X, pp. 335-337), which P. cites, Luther indeed calls A. "that damned, conceited, deceiving pagan", namely with respect to particular doctrines, such as Aristotle's denial of the immortality of the soul. Luther wishes that the books *Physicorum*, *Metaphysicae*, *de Anima*, *Ethicorum*, would be avoided, but concerning the books on "*Logica, Rhetorica, Poetica*" he urges that they be "kept, or brought into another, short form, and are usefully read to teach young people to speak and preach well". After creating the contrary impression, Dr. Pelikan has to admit Luther's "dependence upon philosophy, and Aristotelian philosophy at that." (p. 13). The accompanying footnote casually admits that Luther "endorses Aristotle's logical writings." (p. 125, n.49). He admits, "nevertheless that the Reformer was competent in the use of Aristotelian logic and that he acknowledged it as valid." (p. 13). It appears almost as if, upon writing pp. 10-11, Dr. P. reverses himself in his admissions on p. 13. But then the book proceeds cheerfully as if those admissions had never been made.

One might well ask: what is the point of saying that Luther was "against Aristotle"? If this refers to Aristotle as teacher of philosophical doctrines on such matters as immorality, etc., then Melanchthon and Lutheran Orthodoxy are just as much "against Aristotle". But if it refers to Aristotle's logic, then the claim is admittedly false. Yet the whole Luther-Melanchthon antithesis is based on this assumption!

Dr. Pelikan ambiguously uses the term "Aristotelian philosophy" to denote both doctrinal content (corresponding to the *usus rationis magisterialis*) and logical method (corresponding to the *usus ministerialis*). This creates confusion and incidentally hides the fallacy of his argument.

Dr. Pelikan repeats the cliché about Luther not being a "systematician". One only has to read Luther's violent attack, in his *De Servo Arbitrio*, on Erasmus' agnosticism, to know that Luther was by no means a dreamy Platonic "existentialist", but a stubborn "dogmatist of the dogmatists". To the sophisticated Erasmus, who was shocked at Luther's uncivilized dogmatism, Luther replied in unmistakable language:

"...you say that you find so little satisfaction in assertions that you would readily take up the Sceptics' position wherever the inviolable authority of Holy Scripture and the Church's decisions permit: though you gladly submit your judgment to these authorities in all that they lay down, whether you follow it or not...To take no pleasure in assertions is not the mark of a Christian heart; indeed, one must delight in assertions to be a Christian at all. (Now, lest we be misled by words, let me say here that by 'assertion' I mean staunchly holding your ground, stating your position, confessing it, defending it and reserving in it unvanquished...And I am talking about the assertion of what has been delivered to us from above in the Sacred Scriptures...) Away, now, with Skeptics and Academics from the company of us Christians; let us have men who assert, men twice as inflexible as very Stoics!..Nothing is more familiar or characteristic among Christians than assertions. Take away assertions, and you take away Christianity...What Christian can endure the idea that we should deprecate assertions? That would be denying all religion and piety in one breath asserting that religion and piety and all dogmas are just nothing at all...The Holy Spirit is no Sceptic, and the things He has written in our hearts are not doubts or opinions, but assertions-surer and more certain than sense and life itself." (*The Bondage of the Will*, London: James Clarke & Co. Ltd, pp. 66 ff.)

But what of the Luther-Melanchthon antithesis? Dr. Pelikan admits that Luther reserved "his highest praise...for Melanchthon's *Loci Communes of 1521* and succeeding years. He called it the best book ever written since the Holy Scriptures and urged that the Holy Scriptures should be interpreted according to the Loci. In a moment of extravagance he even suggested that the Loci were worthy of being admitted into the canon" (p. 25).

Are we seriously expected to believe that Luther was such a dunce as not to see, without the aid of From Luther to Kierkegaard, "'the Melanchthonian blight,' the description of faith in mental or intellectual terms,"(p. 27) or "the fact...that Melanchthon's view of justification was a caricature of that of Paul and Luther" (p. 42), etc., etc., *ad nauseam*?

It is quite evident that Dr. Pelikan's repeated laments over stating the "faith in intellectual terms" , etc. refer to the insistence of Lutheran Orthodoxy upon a certain corpus doctrinae, i.e. a series of doctrinal propositions whose correctness is guaranteed by Scripture. In this Orthodoxy differed IN NO WISE from Luther, as even the quotes adduced above show. Lutheranism never insisted that faith IS assent, as Dr. Pelikan pretends, but it did insist that while faith is essentially *fiducia cordis*, it is also *assensus*. The whole thing is quite Scriptural, for "how shall they believe in him (*fiducia*) of whom (*assensus*) they have not heard?" Romans 10. On pp. 58-59, Dr. Pelikan attacks, under the guise of Melanchthonian intellectualism, the Christian doctrine, and Luther's doctrine of certainty. The success of the attack is purely superficial, being contingent upon ambiguity of expression, and a tendential representation of the Orthodox position.

Half-Truth

(3) Dr. Pelikan in several places plays fast and loose with the Orthodox position in order to discredit it. For instance, in his discussion of the *ar-*

53

ticuli mixti, he conveniently fails to note that the Orthodox theologians do NOT assert that faith merely completes what natural knowledge has left incomplete, as Dr. Pelikan implies. Rather, Quenstedt writes: (I, 242) (the *articuli mixti*), "although they may be known in some degree from the light of nature, are nevertheless purely matters of faith, in so far as they are known by divine revelation;...Yet all such things as may be known to some extent by the light of nature, are not matters of faith so far as they are apprehended by the aid of the light of nature, but in as far as they are apprehended by the aid of divine revelation." And Hollaz (45): "No article of faith formally considered, so far as it is an article of faith, is mixed; inasmuch as all articles of faith are dependent on divine revelation, and therefore, with respect to their formal object, are not naturally apprehended." Schmid, *Doctrinal Theology*, pp. 95-96.

Un-Truth

(4) By far the most serious and objectionable feature of the book is the theory, stated on p. 113, that "a repristination of classical Lutheran Orthodoxy was impossible after Kant; he had destroyed the epistemological presuppositions upon which Orthodoxy had built its system. For that reason the attempts that were made to repristinate Orthodoxy failed to produce a lasting theology."

So the Missouri Synod (Walther's, etc., theology was known as "Repristinations theologie") failed to "produce a lasting theology". But this is by the way. The important thing is Kant's alleged destruction of Orthodoxy's epistemological presuppositions.

What did Kant destroy? He "destroyed" the customary "proofs" for the existence of God and denied that theological truths could be rationally demonstrated. But how does this alter or "destroy" any basic presuppositions of Orthodoxy? To be sure, the Orthodox theologians had used the customary "proofs" , perhaps more in the sense of "arguments" than "'proofs", properly speaking. But they explicitly assert that no part of theological truth rests on rational demonstration. Scripture is accepted not because it can be demonstrated that this acceptance is a logical necessity, but because it is a natural consequence of faith in Christ. Philosophically speaking, then, the doctrine that Scripture is the verbally inspired, inerrant Word of God and as such the only source and norm of truth, i.e. of doctrinal propositions, is PURELY AN ASSUMPTION, BECAUSE FAITH IS AN ASSUMPTION. It is true that since the Christian faith is true and correct, therefore all reality in the Universe, when properly understood by human reason, must corroborate and point to Christianity. Therefore Christian apologetics has the legitimate right and duty to show that arguments from human experience against the Christian faith are not necessarily true. The Christian knows that such arguments CANNOT be true, but the most he can usually demonstrate to the unbeliever is that they do not HAVE TO BE true. If men use their perverse reason to deny the existence of God, then this does not mean that the existence of God is not clearly evidenced in nature, or that he that saith, "there is no God" is NOT a fool. Therefore Christian theology has a perfect right to maintain that the existence of God is clear from nature, and that those who deny it are misusing reason. But this is maintained from theology's OWN vantage-point and cannot be imposed upon those who by sophistry and a false use of reason remove; themselves from the influence of the truth.

Once it is admitted that the unconditional submission which the Church accords the Bible as God's Word is PURELY A MATTER OF FAITH , i.e. from the point of view of natural philosophy merely AN ASSUMPTION,—and this admission would in fact be demanded by it—then the whole "epistemological problem" is solved and the "epistemological presuppositions" are quite securely removed beyond the reaches of Kant or any other would-be "destroyer". For can Kant deny the POSSIBILITY that this assumption of faith is correct? Obviously not. And it would certainly follow that if one accepts the fact of a verbally inspired and inerrant message or revelation from God, one certainly cannot accept cynical and skeptical views of the nature and reliability of language itself. One could not, for instance, attempt to penetrate behind the Scriptural language to the "realities themselves" or to some imagined "more basic" or "underlying" entities, because one would have to recognize that the Scripture is the ABSOLUTE on the level of language, behind which there is nothing but abortive speculation. From this preserve and deliver us, good Lord!

GOTTES WORT UND LUTHER'S LEHR'
VERGEHET NUN UND NIMMERMEHR!

Christian News, October 7, 1963

1. Who published from Luther to Kierkegaard? ____.
2. Jaroslav Pelikan began this book when he was teaching at ____ and completed it when he was teaching at ____.
3. Pelikan's book might well have been titled ____.
4. What did the publication of Pelikan's book by CPH show? ____.
5. Pelikan is co-editor of the 56 volume ____.
6. From Luther to Kierkegaard lacks thorough ____.
7. How does Pelikan misrepresent the interrelations between Luther, Melanchthon, and Aristotle? ____.
8. Did Luther have little or no use for Aristotle? ____.
9. Luther: "Take away ____ and you take away Christianity."
10. Luther insisted that faith is essential ____ but also ____.
11. What is the most serious and objectionable feature of Pelikan's book? ____.
12. According to Pelikan the Missouri Synod failed to produce a ____.
13. Christian theology has the perfect right to maintain that the existence of God is clear from ____.
14. ____ is the absolute on the level of language.

MARQUART ON FRANCIS SCHAEFER

A review of Francis Schaeffer, *Escape From Reason* (London: Inter Varsity Press, 1968) (Available from Christian News). *The God Who Is There* (London: Hodder and Stoughton, 1968) (Available from Christian News).

***

"Man is dead. God is dead. Life has become meaningless existence, man a cog in a machine. The only way of escape lies in a non-rational fantasy world of experience, drugs, absurdity, pornography, an elusive 'final experience', madness...If this is the twentieth-century mentality, how did it come about? And how can the Christian faith be made meaningful today? In this highly original book Dr. Schaeffer traces the way in which art and philosophy have reflected the dualism in Western thinking introduced at the time of the Renaissance. Today this dualism is expressed in a despair of rationality and an escape into a non-rational world which alone offers hope. It is shown in literature, art and music, theatre and cinema, television and popular culture."

These sentences from the back cover of *Escape From Reason* pretty well sum up Schaeffer's basic point.

Reason gone berserk

Time was when it was fashionable to sneer at Christianity for not being rational enough. Today Reason itself has fallen into confusion of tongues, and Christianity is blamed for being too rational! How are the mighty fallen! "He that sitteth in the heavens shall laugh: the Lord shall have them in derision" (Ps. 2:4)!

What has happened, according to Schaeffer, is that Reason, having begun with a proud unilateral declaration of independence, has ended by abolishing itself. The persistent attempt to over-reach itself has resulted in a fatal rupture. Reason, having questioned everything, finally had to question itself.

Schaeffer sees Thomas Aquinas and Hegel-Kierkegaard as representing the crucial turning points in the history of Western thought, which led to the present dilemma.

At first sight it seems a bit odd to make that towering giant of lucid rationality, Thomas Aquinas, responsible for the current irrationalism and anti-intellectualism. The trouble, says Schaeffer, is that Aquinas, unlike the Bible and the Reformation, underestimated the effect of sin on the human mind.

This optimism about the capabilities of reason led Aquinas to assign to it too independent a role. The result *was* that reason, in principle freed from revelation in one area, began to conquer other areas, and finally insisted on its own sole supremacy.

In the succeeding centuries reason pursued the goal of providing, alone and without any assistance from revelation, a complete and rationally coherent and satisfying explanation of the universe and of man's place

56

in it.

By Hegel's time (1770-1831) quite a number of competing and conflicting rational explanations of reality had been proposed. There was no argument about whether reason could draw a circle including all reality. The only argument was over just where that circle ought to the drawn. But Hegel undermined this view. In place of the old idea of truth (if A is true, then it's opposite, non-A, is false) Hegel brought in a kind of non-stop triangular motion, now known as dialectic:

A, the thesis, is challenged by B, the antithesis, and the ensuing struggle results in a synthesis C, which in turn becomes the new thesis, etc. This "eternal triangle" did away with absolute truth (not in Hegel's mind, but as a historical consequence) and paved the way for modern pragmatic and relativistic ideas.

Despair and Drugs

This point in the history of ideas Schaeffer calls "the line of despair." He means that at this point reason despaired of finding a unified, rational explanation for everything. From now on reason deals more and more with details and particulars, leaving the great questions of meaning unanswered. These basic issues are now left to intuition, experience, poetry, art, in short, to non-reason.

The first man to cross the line of despair, says Schaeffer, was Kierkegaard, who thus became the father of both secular and religious existentialism. The basic idea is that reason cannot contribute anything of real importance. Meaning, faith can be wrested from the universe only by a non-rational "leap," a decision of the will.

One might think that logical positivism and analytical philosophy are diametrically opposed to the existentialism of men like Jaspers, Sartre, and Heidegger. Schaeffer traces some surprising connections. He shows that for all its emphasis on logic and reason, analytical philosophy too abandons ultimate issues to non-reason. Thus Aldous Huxley, in the last chapter of The Humanist Frame (London: Allen and Unwin, 1961), advocated the use of drugs to attain the "first-order experience," that is, insight into the real nature of things. Timothy Leary relates the L.S.D. experience to the mysticism of the *Tibetan Book of the Dead*.

> Thus he shows that the desire for, and the form of, this experience changes very little from West to East. Whether it is the existentialist speaking, or Aldous Huxley, or Eastern mysticism, we find a uniform need for an irrational experience to make some sense of life. Their views have brought them to a wall and by an unrelated leap of faith they hope to clear the wall. . . Each case involves a non-rational leap of faith (The God Who Is There, pp. 27-28).

In this connection Schaeffer also quotes an anonymous "drug psalm":

> King Heroin is my shepherd, I shall always want. He maketh me to lie down in the gutters. He leadeth me beside the troubled waters. He destroyeth my soul .

"Murder without guilt. Love without meaning"

So screamed the ads for Antonioni's *Blow-Up* in the London Underground. And so the philosophy of meaninglessness reaches the masses, and brainwashes them. Schaeffer believes that the philosophy of meaninglessness and despair affected first art, then music, then general culture, and finally theology. A striking example from music is John Cage, who "composed" by tossing coins. He meant to express meaninglessness in his music. Yet in real life, for example in his hobby of mushroom picking, he found that this philosophy didn't work (*The God Who Is There*, p.73)

About films Schaeffer writes:

> We usually divide cinema and television programmes into two classes — good and bad. The term 'good' as used here means 'technically good' and does not refer to morals. The 'good' pictures are the serious ones, the artistic ones; the ones with good shots. The 'bad' are simply escapist, romantic, only for entertainment. But if we examine them with care we will notice that the 'good' pictures are actually the worst pictures. The escapist film may be horrible in some ways but the so-called 'good' pictures of recent years have almost all been developed by men holding the modern philosophy of meaninglessness. This does not imply they have ceased to be men of integrity, but it does mean that the films they produce are tools for teaching their beliefs (ibid., p. 41).

A good example is Bergman's *The Silence*:

> *The Silence* is a series of snapshots with immoral and pornographic themes. The camera just takes them without any comment. 'Click, Click, Click, cut!' That is all there is. Life is like that: unrelated, having no meaning as well as no morals (ibid., p. 42).

Readers of certain university publications will make their own applications!

Theology: lagging behind

> "Theology has been last for a long time. It is curious to me, in studying this whole cultural drift, that so many pick up the latest theological fashion and hail it as something new. But in fact, what the new theology is now saying has already been said previously in each of the other disciplines" (ibid., p. 16).

The escape from reason that has become so fashionable in theology after Barth is not a heroic return to the New Testament, but a capitulation to the prevailing mentality. Scripture, truth, doctrine, in short, everything objective, is surrendered to secular, critical reason, and "theology" wings its merry way into a foggy fantasy-land of irrational verbosity. Clarity and definition are shunned like the plague, and in place of the New Testament's insistence on the importance of the right teaching of the Gospel (St. Matthew 28: 19,20; Rom. 16:17; Gal. 1:6-8; I Tim. 6:2ff., etc.) we get the trendy jargon about "encounters," "personal truth," "Christocentricity," and the like.

Actually, any "Christ" torn away from the Biblical context in its entirety, is not the Jesus of the New Testament but a human figment. Christ and the Bible stand and fall together. The fashionable notion that it is possible to retain Christ while sacrificing the Bible to "scientific" or "historical" criticism, is a shallow, lazy evasion. And because this point of view is really an escape from reason, it deeply resents and dreads anything to do with logic and rational clarity. This is denounced as "rationalism." Indeed, logic is regarded as the Original Sin! This is, literally, Heidegger's doctrine:

> "It is intriguing that the new Heidegger, as he changed his position, tried to get a historic Fall into his new system. He says there was a Golden Age (before this Fall) at the time of the pre-Socratic Greeks; and then Aristotle, and those who followed him, fell. Their fall was that they began to think rationally. . . In Heidegger's desperate theory, Aristotle takes the place of Adam, as the one who fell, and it does appear as if Heidegger sees himself as the one who will save" (*The God Who Is There*, p. 185, n.5).

Francis Schaeffer's books can help modern Christians to understand the age in which they live, to see beyond symptoms to underlying causes. Shallow mini-gospels cannot cope with the chaos of our time. But real Christianity, which is not ashamed of its intellectual substance, is surprisingly relevant to the real needs and problems of space-age people!

Christian News, October 29, 1973

1. What is Francis Schaeffer's main point in Escape from Reason? ____.
2. Reason has gone ____.
3. Hegel's "eternal triangle" did away with ____.
4. According to Schaeffer, the first man to cross the line of despair was

____.
5. Aldous Huxley in the last chapter of The Humanist Frame advocated the use of ____.
6. Schaeffer believed that the philosophy of meaninglessness and despair affected ____.
7. Any Christ torn away from the Biblical context in its entirety is not the Jesus of ____ but a ____.
8. Christ and the Bible ____ and ____together.
9. ____ is regarded as the original sin.
10. Francis Schaeffer's books can help modern man to ____.

SANCTIFYING AN UNHOLY CAUSE

Reverend Sir,

I have just read, in your April 20 number, that pathetic "notice" against LUTHERAN NEWS, for which the Missouri Synod's "Council of Administrators" have dared even to exploit Maundy Thursday—hoping apparently to sanctify an unholy cause with a holy day!

Actually, you should feel very pleased about this notice, because it confirms that what you have been saying is true and unanswerable. At least that must be the presumption until the contrary is proved.

To understand the implications of that "notice," let us imagine the following situation: A public-spirited citizen claims to become aware of the existence of a corrupt political machine in his area, and starts a protest movement, which publishes and meticulously documents specific charges. There-upon the machine publishes a notice in the press:

1. That irresponsible paper is not the official voice of the Organization, but a private venture.

2. The editor is not an accredited member of the Organization.

3. The supporters of the editor have been expelled from the Organization.

4. Despite the Organizations explicit orders, the protest movement continues to annoy citizens, press, and government officials with unsolicited communications!

Such a notice may serve the purpose of warning the "faithful" but anyone not bribed or intimidated by the Organization would immediately brand such a statement as a clumsy admission of guilt.

Without wishing to impute to the gentlemen concerned—many of whom acted perhaps with incomplete knowledge and understanding—any similarities to political gangsterism, the fact nevertheless remains that in the minds of the unprejudiced they have done their cause only harm by trying to meet arguments with insults.

AN INCREDIBLE ACT OF SECTARIANISM

As for the "expulsion" of your Congregation, this was an incredible act of sectarianism and schism on the part of the perpetrators . Imagine responsible servants of Christ, spiritual heirs of Paul and Luther, even toying with the idea of cutting off pulpit and altar fellowship FOR WHAT IS ADMITTEDLY ONLY A DIFFERENCE ABOUT HUMAN PROCE-DURE, NOT ABOUT DIVINELY GIVEN DOCTRINE OR PRACTICE! That is the very heart and essence of that "schism and sectarianism" against which the Missouri Synod is constitutionally bound to provide "a united defence" (Art. III, 1)!

How eloquently did not Dr. Walther and the others argue, at the founding of the Synod in 1847, that, unlike the liberal Eastern synods the Missouri Synod was to have no power whatever to bind anyone to anything beyond the clear Word of God! It was specifically guaranteed,

60

again and again, that the Synod would not have the slightest power to compel obedience to any human regulations! And now you have been expelled—for daring to claim and act upon your God—given evangelical freedom, guaranteed to you in the Missouri Synod's constitution.

You have been expelled for accepting evangelically and constructively the challenge of a situation forced upon you "un-solicited." You have been expelled—by those who continue, by their words and actions, to coddle, defend and fellowship representatives of false doctrine within and without the Missouri Synod—because you refused to submit your consciences to orders which were ADMITTEDLY only of human, and not of divine authority! Where are the limits to such ecclesiastical arrogance, such utterly unevangelical, sectarian tyranny?

Continue to fight this thing, boldly and bravely, in the name of God and of His one holy Church!

K. Marquart

Christian News, June 15, 1964

1. Dr. Marquart said that the expulsion of Trinity Lutheran Church of New Haven, Missouri was an incredible act of ____.
2. Marquart encouraged the editor of Christian News to ____.

Editor's Note: The April 20, 1964 Christian News reprinted from the April 14, 1964 Lutheran Witness the official notice on "Lutheran News." It was signed by:

Arthur M. Ahlschwede, Chairman
   Division of Higher Education
Milton Carpenter, Chairman
   Division of Finance
Otto A. Dorn, Chairman
   Division of Church Literature
Oliver R. Harms, Chairman
   Division of Doctrine and Church Relations
John E. Herrmann, Chairman
   Division of Special Ministries
William H. Hillmer, Chairman
   Division of Missions
Arthur L. Miller, Chairman
   Division of Parish Education and Services
Martin W. Mueller, Chairman
   Division of Communications and Public Relations
Raymond C. Rauscher, Chairman
   Division of Controllership
Roland P. Wiederaenders, Chairman
   Division of Church Government
Henry F. Wind, Chairman
   Division of Social Action and Welfare
Walter F. Wolbrecht, Chairman
   Council of Administrators

SPECIAL PRESIDENTIAL COMMITTEE DISAGREES WITH FT. WAYNE PROFESSOR MARQUART: ST. LOUIS SEMINARY LOST CASE VS. OTTEN

Professor Kurt Marquart of Concordia Seminary, Ft. Wayne, told a Special Presidential Committee asked to deal with Concordia Seminary, St. Louis, vs. Herman Otten case that the seminary failed to show just cause for refusing to certify Otten for the ministry. The committee was formed in response to a resolution adopted at the LCMS's 1995 convention.

Many regard Marquart as one of the leading theologians in the U.S. The Board of Appeals of the Lutheran Church ordered the St. Louis Seminary to show cause for refusing to certify Otten. Marquart told the committee: "The case ended in a 5-5 tie or non-decision. Anywhere else but in the Soviet Union and in other dark corners of unchallenged bureaucratic arrogance, it would have been self-evident that the seminary had failed to show cause."

When Otten asked Dr. James Kalthoff why the Special Presidential Committee took issue with Marquart's statement, he said that he could not answer any questions about the committee's report. Marquart was a counselor for Otten in the case. They had been roommates at the St. Louis Seminary. Dr. Siegbert Becker, a professor at Concordia Teachers College, River Forest, and Rev. H. W. Niewald, pastor of Bethlehem Lutheran Church, New Haven, were Otten's other counselors.

The Special Presidential Committee says in its 41-page report, published in this issue of CN, that the meaning of the 5-5 ruling has not been clarified even though the LCMS's Commission on Appeals ruled in 1984 that the 5-5 ruling meant that the seminary failed to show cause and that Otten was the prevailing party. The LCMS's Handbook says that such rulings are binding. The Special Presidential Committee faults Otten for failing to ask for a rehearing. Otten and his counselors did not ask for any rehearing because they accepted the ruling of the Board of Appeals. Why should the winner ask for a rehearing?

Marquart wrote to Dr. James Kalthoff, chairman of the Special Presidential Committee on April 26, 1996:

The Rev. Dr. James Kalthoff,
President
Missouri District, LC-MS , and Chairman
Special Presidential Committee
3558 S. Jefferson Avenue
St. Louis, MO 63118

Dear Brother Kalthoff,
Upon your shoulders, and your Committee's, rests the enormous bur-

den of advising President Barry as to the best evangelical, God-pleasing treatment for an open wound of long standing on our Synodical body. I begged both Presidents Jack Preus and Ralph Bohlmann to find a solution for the vexing matter of Pastor Herman Otten's status, before the human cost to all concerned would escalate further. I did not write to Dr. Barry because I knew that his pastoral, evangelical heart needed no prodding from me. And now the matter is before your Committee.

In approaching your Committee through you as its Chairman, I do not presume to suggest any specific form of settlement, nor have I the call or the wisdom to do so.

There are, however, two issues in respect of which I am conscience-bound to ask that the Committee be perfectly clear. One is the nature and outcome of the original Otten vs. Seminary case (1960), in which I happened to have in active part. The other is the relationship obtaining in principle between ecclesiastical rules or bylaws on the one hand, and justice and charity on the other.

Ad(1)

I do not have a copy of the official record. But I remember the crucial events and issues as vividly as if the whole thing had taken place last week. As a young pastor just out of the seminary, I had suddenly, with fear and trembling, to act as "trial lawyer" for Herman Otten before the Synodical Board of Appeals—with nothing but an odd episode or two of Perry Mason to supply my legal "education." I noted with distaste then as I do now that the Seminary did not trust itself to confront two of its own recent young students, but chose to hide behind its lawyers, who conducted the Seminary's entire case for them! The record places the following points beyond dispute:

(a) The case was defined, by the then Synodical Board of Appeals, as a "show cause" action: Concordia Seminary, St. Louis, was ordered to show cause why Herman Otten should not be certified for the ministry. It was made crystal-clear at the outset that the burden of proof rested on the Seminary, and the Seminary's representatives happily accepted that burden.

(b) The Seminary was anxious (and with good reason) to avoid the issue of the truth or falsity of Herman Otten's reports. Therefore his "sin" was defined very narrowly as consisting in his having reported classroom teachings, in some cases, on the say-so of others, without having spoken in person with the professors concerned. Regardless of the truth or falsity of the allegations, the Seminary argued, such secondhand reports of public classroom statements are, absent prior personal verification, in and of themselves (*"per se"*) always sin.

(c) Dean of Students L. Wuerffel testified that the Faculty's Discipline Committee had found against Herman Otten and recommended to the Faculty that he not be certified. In cross-examination I put the following question to Dean Wuerffel: "Did the members of the Faculty personally verify the Discipline Committee's charges with Herman Otten, before voting to condemn him?" After several attempts to have the question answered, the Dean had to reply: "No, they did not." I permit myself a personal digression, since the transcript will not show this: At this exchange some lawyers on the Board were grinning broadly, for they understood very well the fatal self-contradiction now manifest in the Seminary's case.

(d) The case ended in a 5-to-5 tie or non-decision. Anywhere else but in the Soviet Union and in other dark corners of unchallenged bureaucratic arrogance, it would have been self-evident that the Seminary had failed to show cause. It must also be remembered that

(e) Herman Otten had not published his reports about the Seminary situation, but had merely given them confidentially to high Synodical officials at their request. It was they who made them public.

(f) The Seminary's officials refused to accept as adequate Herman Otten's several profuse apologies, but tried to force him to agree to their unproven "per se" theory, which his conscience would not allow. Two salient points were added by subsequent history:

(g) The whole "Seminex" development vindicated Pastor Otten's concerns many times over. The vendetta against him now stood revealed as the typical reaction of entrenched interests to an unwelcome whistle-blower. This corrupt suppression of justice should have been officially reversed the moment "Seminex" had departed. The great Hermann Sasse, observing the situation from distant Australia, wrote in 1970: "Somebody should rise and publicly thank Herman Otten for his brave fight. We all were sometimes not fully agreed with him. He has made blunders. But why was it left to a young pastor to speak where others should have spoken?" (*Christian News*, 2 March 1970).

(h) On 26 November, 1984, the Synod's Commission on Appeals, in response to an earlier request by then Seminary President Ralph Bohlmann, ruled that the 1960 tie-vote had "resulted in a decision against the Faculty and Board of Control of Concordia Seminary, St. Louis, Missouri, since they failed to meet their stipulated burden of proof and Herman Otten shall be considered to have been the prevailing party." I reported this in print (*Affirm*, April, 1985), under the heading "Justice Delayed . . .," and with the comment: "Such a decision tends to confirm one's confidence in the integrity of our synodical appeals process."

It is now over a decade later—and three and a half decades after the original case—yet the Synodical machinery still grinds on in deaf disregard of these truths, which stand, unimpeachable, in the broadest light of day.

Ad (2)

You have no need for me to draw out the implications of Our Lord's admonition: "Judge not according to the appearance, but judge righteous judgment" (St. John 7:24). Yet the existence in our church of a rigid juridicalism, which mistakes Synodical bylaws for iron-clad canon law, prompts me to offer the briefest of observations on this score. Forgive me if I'm carrying coals to Newcastle!

Contrary to the popular impression that, by analogy to the secular separation of powers, conventions "legislate" for our church, the fact is that according to Lutheran conviction neither the church as a whole nor anyone in it has any power to "legislate" anything. Luther's passionate eloquence on the subject is well known. Closer to home, Pieper insisted that "God has not invested the Church, or individuals in the Church, with legislative authority; on the contrary, here the rule is: 'One is your Master, even Christ; and all ye are brethren' (Matt. 23.8)" [*Christian Dogmatics* 111:432].

Walther took pride in the fact that our Synod claimed no other powers or authority than that of the Word of God. Otherwise, he prophesied, "[o]ur chief battle would soon center about the execution of manufactured, external human ordinances and institutions and would swallow up the true blessed battle for the real treasure of the church, for the purity and unity of doctrine" (*Concordia Journal*, Sept. 1976, p. 203). He quoted Luther regarding consistories that had assumed coercive powers: "We must tear the consistories to pieces, for we do not by any means want to have the lawyers and the pope in them" (*The Form of a Christian Congregation*, p. 11).

Walther and Pieper both stressed that neither majorities nor minorities have any inherent right to prevail, but that faith and love must decide everything. Even "parliamentary rules," i.e. Robert's Rules of Order, may not be applied legalistically to "limit free debate" or generally be "employed in a loveless manner against those who are not so well versed in parliamentary procedure" (Pieper, p. 434).

Bylaws, then are not "laws" in any strict sense at all. They are, like liturgical details, *adiaphora*, or rules of good order which we freely impose on ourselves, and to which we gladly submit for the sake of love and unity. But if faith, or love, or justice demand it, the human rules must be changed or suspended. In the church human procedure must always yield to divine substance, and legal formality to normal obligation. The letter must submit to the spirit, not the other way around, or we cease to be evangelical.

Not being a canonist, I shall not adduce many precedents. I do want to cite only two instances which in my view illustrate our church's evangelical approach to bylaws which I have been trying to describe.

In 1874 the Synod resolved:

Whereas the whole churchly authority of the congregations is represented in the Synod when it holds its sessions, and accordingly the General Synod must be conceded the right, in case of necessity, to circumvent the mode of election prescribed as the rule by the Constitution:

Resolved, that the General Synod reserve for itself the right for extraordinary cases, when it is in session, itself to conduct elections for the filling of teaching positions in its institutions, but with the proviso that elections conducted in such cases must be submitted to the congregations for ratification (1874 *Proceedings*, p. 59, my translation).

A hundred years later, in adopting revised bylaws governing Colloquy procedures. Synod expressly provided exemptions and exceptions for "Seminex" and Saskatoon graduates (1975 *Proceedings*, pp. 143-144).

It is theologically and historically false therefore to say that Synod is bound hand and foot to existing regulations, and cannot make special provisions for special situations. God grant you and your Committee the grace to pursue a God-pleasing solution in that sacred "liberty wherewith Christ hath made us free" (Gal. 5:1).

Permit me to conclude with something I was told some years ago by someone in a position to know. When the late Dr. Oliver Harms was trying, on behalf of the Synod, to come to amicable terms with Dr. Brux, who had been dismissed many years earlier from his missionary duties in India, he asked Dr. Brux: "In these past 30 years, did anyone from the Synod ever approach you, or inquire how you were?" "No, no one ever came," replied Dr. Brux. Then a shocked Dr. Harms said to his assistant: "We must never let this happen again." The person who told me this added: "I believe he was talking about Herman Otten."

You will not mind, I am sure, if I send a copy of this to Synodical Vice-President Dr. Wallace Schulz as well, who is on your Committee, and for whom I also have a high regard.

Wishing you and yours all the riches of this holy Paschal season,
Cordially yours,
K. Marquart
Ft. Wayne, Indiana

Christian News, March 10, 1997

1. Dr. Marquart had been a ____ for Otten in the Seminary vs. Otten case.
2. What was Marquart's only "legal training?" ____.
3. Concordia Seminary hid behind its ____.
4. The seminary was anxious to avoid ____.
5. The seminary failed to ____.
6. The whole Seminex development vindicated ____.
7. What did Herman Sasse observe from Australia? ____.
8. In 1984 the LCMS's Commission on Appeals ruled that the 1960 tie vote resulted in ____.

FIRST AMENDMENT IMMUNITY

Affirm, 1991

Of late Synodical representatives have been following a most peculiar line in court cases. They have been claiming virtually total immunity for church officials from legal action by parties who regard themselves as wronged or victimized by such officials. The idea is that any disputes in the church involve religious issues and therefore fall under the taboo of the First Amendment. In one recent case, which fortunately Synodical officials lost, they argued, for example: "The issues surrounding the doctrine of the call, the authority of various committees, commissions and officers in the Synod and the interpretation of synodical bylaws and procedures are not within the Court's subject matter jurisdiction. They should properly be resolved by the church, not the state". Well, the doctrine of the call, yes, that is hardly a matter for the courts. But what is so arcanely "religious" about the bylaws, of all things? These bylaws define and establish contractually enforceable relations and obligations. There is precious little theology in them—would that there were more!

Whether Synodical administrators may thumb their noses at final decisions rendered by their synodical Commission on Appeals is something which is presumably clearly settled in the bylaws. At least the question whether this issue is or is not clearly settled has nothing peculiarly "religious" about it. Courts of law routinely decide much more complicated matters than that. They are perfectly capable of handling such questions without the aid of ecclesiastical soothsayers. Or are our bylaws so badly written that they require arcane hermeneutical devices like Joseph Smith's 'peepstone' for their decipherment?

The effect of this bizarre exploitation of the First Amendment would be a mischievous new "benefit of Clergy," under which church bureaucracies could abuse their powers with impunity, so long as they could maintain effective control of their corporate structures. Given that, they could inflict whatever injustices they liked on the rank and file under their control, secure in the knowledge that the courts had to keep "hands off" in the name of the First Amendment! A fine case of "freedom of religion" that would be!

Holy Finances?

If the argument holds for church bylaws, it must hold for finances as well. Church officials charged with embezzlement could then claim that they used special "holy accounting" methods, which secular courts could not possibly comprehend, and over which they could have no jurisdiction under the First Amendment! The mind boggles at the possibilities.

Kurt Marquart

Christian News, March 25, 1991

1. Do all disputes in the Church fall under the taboo of the First Amendment? ____.

2. How much theology is there in many of the by-laws? ____.
3. May Synodical administrators thumb their noses at opinions of the LCMS's Commission on Appeals? ____.
4. What was Joseph Smith's Peepstone? ____.
5. Church officials charged with embezzlement could claim ____.

LEADERS SELECT WEISHEIT
TO BE BANQUET SPEAKER

Rev. Eldon Weisheit will be banquet speaker at the International Convention of the Lutheran Laymen's League in Phoenix, Arizona on August 1. Weisheit was associate editor of the *Lutheran Witness* from 1971 through 1975 and since 1969 he has served on the special script committee for Lutheran Television. From 1972 through 1975 he was acting editor of *Advance Magazine*. He is third vice-president of the English District of the Lutheran Church Missouri Synod. Weisheit has authored 16 books dealing with children's messages, the history of the LCMS, poetry, counseling, and homiletics. He is listed in "Who's Who in American Religion" and "Contemporary American Authors." Weisheit is a theological liberal who sided with the liberals in Seminex during the doctrinal controversy which rocked the LCMS. He attacked the inerrancy of Holy Scripture in material published by the LCMS's Board of Youth Ministry (See *The Christian News Encyclopedia*, p. 1255).

Weisheit is the author of a pro-abortion book published by The Lutheran Church-Missouri Synod's Concordia Publishing House. Although LCMS officials are pro-life and the LCMS has taken a strong stand against abortion, officials are not disciplining liberals in the synod who allow for abortion. Professor Kurt Marquart said in a review of Weisheit's CPH book published in the Concordia Theological Quarterly: "In language reminiscent of the worst liberationist claptrap, he (Weisheit, ed.) speaks of the 'right' to kill the unborn as 'the freedom that many have struggled for all women to have' (p. 21). Caricaturing the public debate about abortion, Weisheit announces loftily: 'I hope that neither side 'wins'" (p. 70)—as if there could be a middle ground between affirmation and denial of the legal personhood of the unborn!"

Professor Marquart says that "The sad fact is that the controlling ideas of the Weisheit books simply do not represent Christian ethics. Nowhere is there a real sense of horror of abortion as killing, such as has from the beginning characterized the Christian view of life." The Concordia, Ft. Wayne professor concludes his review (reprinted in *The Christian News Encyclopedia*, p. 11):

"The tragedy is that he has become the unwitting victim of perspectives and premises utterly at variance with Christian truth. His priorities have become subtly secularized. Thus, he can be emphatic about the evil of 'sexual maladjustment' (pp. 35-44), but not about the evil of abortion. He concludes: 'I have tried not to demand or plead in this book. But I would do either if it would discourage you from a medically unsafe abortion.' (p. 95). Again, unsanitary surgical procedures are worth warning against; the application of 'meat processing' techniques techniques (McLuhan) to the unborn is not! Already the book has been commended as 'open-ended' in the *Lutheran Women Quarterly* (Fall, 1976, p. 24). Unsuspecting Christian women naturally trust that no deadly poison will be dispensed through church-related publications. The 'open-ended'

Weisheit books constitute in the deepest, biblical sense of that word, a *skandalon*. Good Lord, deliver us!"

"We can look forward to hearing our banquet speaker," says the Rev. William Dingler, director of media services for the International LLL. "Pastor Weisheit is a long-time friend and colleague of the league and has made a distinct contribution to our Gospel outreach through television specials. He always comes up with ingenious ways to communicate the Good News that can be found only in Christ Jesus. His excitement about the Gospel excites others, too, and I'm sure this will be an important part of the entire banquet experience."

Conservative members of the L.L.L. are wondering why their leaders selected a theological liberal to be the banquet speaker at their convention.

Christian News, July 9, 1984

1. Who was Eldon Weisheit? ____.
2. LCMS officials are not disciplining liberals who allow for ____.
3. The "open-ended" Weishet books constitutes ____.

STOP CPH FROM PUBLISHING ABORTION BOOK – "KILLING WITH KINDNESS"

How much longer will it take before Concordia Publishing House stops commending Rev. Eldon Weisheit's Should I Have An Abortion? Lutheran Church — Missouri Synod President Jacob Preus months ago should have urged Dr. Ralph Reinke, President of CPH, to take some decisive action against the book. Preus has done nothing to stop CPH from promoting such anti-scriptural CPH publications as Should I Have An Abortion? and From Out Of The Desert, a CPH sound filmstrip which rejects the Christian doctrine of justification by faith alone. Reinke says that Preus appointed censors approved From Out Of The Desert.

Christian News noted almost a year ago that the Weisheit book allows for the murder of unborn infants. Dr. Paul Kahldahl, a pathologist from Oklahoma City, has shown several times in Christian News that the Weisheit book leaves the door wide open for the killing of unborn infants. Officials of the LCMS and the Board of Directors of CPH have been requested to take some action against the book. The LCMS has adopted an excellent statement opposing abortion, but LCMS pastors and professors are still allowed to promote abortion even when the life of the mother is not in danger. No action is being taken against some Lutheran Hospitals where unborn infants are being murdered. Charges of false doctrine against a pro-abortion LCMS clergyman were ignored by the LCMS President.

The Lutheran Women's Quarterly and even Christianity Today have commended the Weisheit book. Articles by Weisheit continue to appear in the Lutheran Witness. We have asked the editor of the Lutheran Witness if he believes that the LCMS should be broad enough to allow for those who support abortion on demand, but we have received no response. It appears to us that by this time numerous pro-life and anti-abortion articles should have appeared in the LCMS's official publication.

Anyone who checks our indexes for the last ten years will find hundreds of items on abortion. The Lutheran Witness has been almost totally silent on the subject. One brief item by Rev. Sam Nafzger, executive secretary of the LCMS's Commission On Theology, is about the only fine pro-life and anti-abortion statement we have seen in the Lutheran Witness for a long time.

Some officials maintain that only such "ultra" conservatives as the editor of Christian News and Dr. Paul Kaldahl oppose the Weisheit book. We hope that all of Missouri's top officials read Professor Kurt Marquart's "Killing with Kindness" which we are reproducing below from the January, 1977 Concordia Theological Quarterly.

CPH MUST BE STOPPED FROM PUBLISHING ANYTHING WHICH ALLOWS FOR THE KILLING OF UNBORN CHILDREN.

Killing with Kindness

K. MARQUART

January, 1977 CONCORDIA THEOLOGICAL QUARTERLY.

A Review of Eldon Weisheit, *Should I Have An Abortion?* **(Concordia Publishing House, 1976, 101 pages) and** *Abortion? Resources For Pastoral Counseling* **(Concordia Publishing House, 1976, 173 pages).**

Compassion is absolutely central to the practice of Christianity. Cruel, legalistic moralism ill befits a servant of the Good Shepherd—least of all a Lutheran pastor. He is, after all, the administrator not of justice and death, nor of social crusades, but of mercy and divine, eternal life. This evangelical compassion is clearly the approach which Pastor Weisheit intended should shape his whole treatment of the abortion question. His pastoral practice has made him deeply aware of the agonies of individuals actually faced with the problem. But the pastor, above all, dare not be dominated by mere feeling. We must not lose our pastoral heads over our pastoral hearts. Mere fleshly sentiment helps no one.

Weisheit is aware of, even disturbed by this tension. He states in the preface to the longer book—which incorporates the text of the shorter one plus added materials for counselors—that during his year of research away from "frontline counseling" he became "much more anti-abortion." Unfortunately this sobering impact of a more objective look at the nature of abortion was not allowed to prevail at the crucial points of the discussion. Indeed, the author seems so exclusively preoccupied with the woman's distress, and therefore so determined to treat abortion as an open question, that he can no longer deal objectively with the basic facts.

For example, Weisheit repeatedly sets up spurious alternatives, which create the illusion of a responsible middle ground between the two "extremes." It is simply a fiction to suggest that the choice is between "no abortion for any reason" and "any abortion for no reason" (p. 70). To discredit the pro-life movement by identifying it, as Weisheit does here, with the first of these alternatives, is irresponsible. The whole point is that, unlike the abortionists, the pro-lifers distinguish sharply between serious grounds for considering abortion (to save another human life) and frivolous ones (avoidance of embarrassment, inconvenience, etc.). The Human Life Amendment proposed by the National Right to Life organization after a year of painstaking legal work explicitly provides "that nothing in this article shall prohibit a law permitting only those medical procedures required to prevent the death of the mother."

Rendering "no abortion except to prevent the mother's death" as "no abortion for any reason" indicates either gross negligence in reading or else propagandistic intent. Something similar occurs on page 171. Among the books suggested for further reading, Weisheit lists the *Handbook on Abortion* by Dr. and Mrs. J. C. Willke. But then he describes this excellent book as a "hardhitting, emotional . . . attack against abortion under any circumstances." Actually the book is very factual and much less emotional than Weisheit's. And it reprints with full endorsement the Human Life Amendment, including the provision for abortion to save the mother's life! Yet Weisheit sees it as "an extreme position" and says that "the book should not be given to a person who has had or who is considering an abortion"! No such warning is issued against any of the other books listed, the majority of which defend looser views.

The whole sixth chapter, dealing with the divine will, is a disaster. After some preliminaries suggesting that no one can claim to know God's mind on the subject, we read: "The Bible does not say, Thou shalt not commit abortion . . . Some want to make the commandment 'Thou shalt not kill' also read. Thou shalt not have an abortion'"(p. 68). One can hear Hitler caviling:

"It does not say, 'Thou shalt not gas Jews'"! Yet on the same page Weisheit admits quite correctly: "God does speak of life in the womb as being a person"! How then can one honestly avoid the conclusion that abortion is killing? Left without a clear word from God, Weisheit is reduced to waffling vaguely about "love" in the manner of the situationists. And what serious ethic could possibly be built on a concept like "God's advice" (p. 71)? Here the thunder of the Law has been muted into a pitiful psychiatric whimper.

But it is in the next chapter that the book's perversity becomes fully apparent. If an abortionist had set out deliberately to confuse the issues, he could not have done much better than Weisheit's chapter seven. Everything here is in the service of the predetermined conclusion that abortion must remain an open question. "Is the fetus another state of human life similar to the categories baby, child, adolescent, and adult? Or is it a term for prehuman existence, such as male sperm or female egg?" asks Weisheit. But then comes the incredible reply: "There are no simple answers to such questions"! There follow all sorts of red herrings and half-truths designed to insure that by hook or by crook the question shall remain open. If indeed, on Weisheit's own admission, "God does speak of life in the womb as being a person," one would have thought that the issue was settled, finally and categorically. Instead, God's attitude is fleetingly acknowledged and then blithely ignored. Perhaps it was too "theological" to be intruded into a medical chapter. But then at least the known scientific facts should have been objectively stated and honestly faced.

It is simply not true that medically speaking, "there are a number of points in human development that could be regarded as the beginning of life" (p. 77). Particularly since the discovery of DNA there is no excuse for any equivocation on the point that biologically speaking, the fetus is from conception a distinct and unique human life in its own right. Modern knowledge here corrects primitive folklore about "quickening" or about each sperm containing a miniature boy, etc., as well as Darwinian superstitions about "prehuman" stages of development. Weisheit introduces such notions, refutes each of them, also the irrelevant criterion of "viability," but then still treats them as though they were genuine medical grounds for doubting that the fetus is a human being! To inflict such wilful confusions on possibly ill-informed and certainly emotionally distressed women considering abortions borders on the cynical. In view of Weisheit's glib assumption that the fetus is not a psychological person (p. 79), it is instructive to note that the distinguished Professor A. W. Liley of the University of Auckland's Postgraduate School of Obstetrics and Gynecology has explicitly described "The Fetus as a Personality" in a fascinating article under that title in the *Australia and New Zealand Journal of Psychiatry* (1972:6: p. 99).

We have a right to expect more candor and greater perception from Christian counselors than from secular pro-abortionists. Yet in these very respects Weisheit's book contrasts unfavorably with an editorial in the pro-abortion *Journal* of the California State Medical Association (Sept., 1970):

> Since the old ethic has not yet been fully displaced, it has been necessary to separate the idea of abortion from the idea of killing which continues to be socially abhorrent. The result has been a curious avoidance of the scientific fact, which everyone really knows, that human life begins at conception, and is continuous, whether intra- or extra-uterine, until death. The very considerable semantic gymnastics which are required to rationalize abortion as anything but taking a human life would be ludicrous if they were not often put forth under socially impeccable auspices. It is suggested that this schizophrenic sort of subterfuge is necessary because, while a new ethic is being accepted, the old one has not yet been rejected.

Pro-abortion propagandists rely on the sort of confusions fostered by Weisheit's book. They fear and resent—and with good reason!—photographic documentation which cuts through the soothing verbiage to confront people with the startling realities of abortion. For when the average person sees a tiny but perfectly recognizable human being, he will no longer be able to think of it as a shapeless blob or as impersonal "cells" (cf. Weisheit, p. 75). Not surprisingly Weisheit shares the abortionists' disdain of "full color pictures" (p. 171), suggests that open-heart surgery would lie equally upsetting to watch, and declares: "The gory details are not valid reasons to be opposed to abortion" (p. 16). But unlike a severed finger or an excised appendix the sight of babies and parts of babies in disposal bags outrages not our aesthetic sensibilities, but our deepest moral sense. We find the wanton killing of helpless humans abhorrent not because our nerves are failing, but precisely because our conscience is functioning. The only alternative is the cool, scientific objectivity of those terrible Nazi "doctors."

At Nuremberg the legal implications were still clear. Hence Nazi defendants were convicted by American judges on the charge that "protection of the law was denied to unborn children." This attitude has been self-evident in America ever since the enactment, over a hundred years ago, of abortion law reform, which was spearheaded by the American Medical Association and reflected the growing scientific understanding of human reproduction. This too is the background against which the Fourteenth Amendment must be understood. Yet in 1973 the U.S.

Supreme Court formally withdrew the protection of the law from the unborn ("legal personhood does not exist prenatally"). As a result of this relapse into pagan barbarity (Roman law saw the fetus simply as a part of the mother's "viscera"), we now have a topsy-turvy legal system in which it is "unconstitutional" to protect unborn innocents by law from summary execution, while gangsters and murderers are guaranteed "due process." The secular humanism which justifies and motivates this horror is precisely the same sort of "scientific" inhumanity which in the case of Nazi Germany we profess to abhor.

Weisheit, in his sentimental "know-nothingism," sees none of this. In language reminiscent of the worst liberationist claptrap, he speaks of the "right" to kill the unborn as "the freedom that many have struggled for all women to have" (p. 21). Caricaturing the public debate about abortion, Weisheit announces loftily: "I hope that neither side 'wins'" (p. 70) —as if there could be middle ground between affirmation and denial of the legal personhood of the unborn! If even a trained counselor can be as confused about abortion as Weisheit evidently is, how can the individual woman be expected to reach a responsible decision? If respect for life is the cornerstone of civilized law, then the taking of human life cannot be left to the whim of private individuals — least of all to those whose self-interest is most directly involved. We are all only too prone to self-deception, particularly under strong emotional pressure. How many tormented women, desperate for a way out, will find in Weisheit's "compassionate" blurring of moral, medical, and legal absolutes sufficient justification for abortion?

The sad fact is that the controlling ideas of the Weisheit books simply do not represent Christian ethics. No where is there a real sense of horror of abortion as killing, such as has from the beginning characterized the Christian view of life. As Bishop Per Lonning comments on Isaiah 13:18: "What is remarkable in this statement is that the atrocity against the unborn is regarded as even more serious than that perpetrated against the mother. To deny the human being even the right to be born is regarded as the height of barbarity." Such was the respect for the sanctity of unborn life at the time of Christ that entering a Gentile house was considered as defiling one with the seven-day uncleanness contracted by touching a corpse, for the reason that Gentiles practiced abortion, and threw their aborted babies into the drains (Strack-Billerbeck, *Kommentar,* II, p. 830)! The late Dr. H. Sasse has pointed out that "we may assume that murder in the ordinary sense of the word did not occur in the Christian Church. In almost all cases where we hear of murder, abortion is meant" *(The Lutheran,* Australia, 7 Sept. 1970). This is especially convincing when the deadly sin of murder is named together with that of fornication (cf. Rev. 9:21). And the practice of inducing abortions by means of poisons (denounced in the Oath of Hippocrates) must fall under the condemnations of "pharmakeia" (Gal. 5:20).

Weisheit's abortion ethic springs from different sources. He speaks of giving "moral and spiritual guidance" (p. 111). But there is no authoritative word from God on the subject. From this *proton pseudos* it follows

75

that the point is to present to the individual a potpourri of "some say this and some say that" in the hope that a responsible selection will be made: "Theological statements need to lie applied in practical language so the counselee can understand why some people object to abortion and others approve" (p.111)! Indeed, she should realize that some will criticize her for having an abortion, others will criticize her for having a baby." Are both criticisms equally valid? "Help her find what she wants to do," the counselor is told. He should also be prepared with the "objective facts"— including addresses, "cost," and "method" of available abortion services! This is a shocking reminder of Dr. and Mrs. Willke's claim that "almost all 'Clergy Counselling Service' groups and, with few exceptions, also most Planned Parenthood agencies are truly abortion referral groups" (p. 191). Some of them even profiteer financially from this death business; one Planned Parenthood Clergy Counselling group made $300,000 annually from 12,000 "patients" at "$25.00 a throw"!

That many clergy in secularized denominations cannot distinguish between compassion and permissiveness is not surprising. Their outlook is simply that of the "psychiatric ideology" (Szasz), which has so deeply infected the "counselling" movement. As the intimitable Malcolm Muggeridge has put it: "Nietzsche, no Liberal, announced that God was dead; the same Deity's Liberal ministrants today seek to confute Nietzsche by stuffing an empty skin with Freudian entrails." The same destructive ideology is in large measure responsible for that deadly cancer which Solzhenitsyn sees gnawing at the vitals of our civilization: the pragmatic habit of treating the distinction between good and evil as a matter of indifference.

The basic facts of life and death, as regards the unborn, are really crystal clear. And they would never be in controversy were it not for a blinding obsession with sexual "liberation." Reason, science, morality, religion, law —all must yield before the squeals and grunts of the Gadarene stampede: "I'll have my fun, and to hell with anything that gets in the way!" This neo-paganism is, no doubt, as hateful to Pastor Weisheit as it is to this reviewer. The tragedy is that he has become the unwitting victim of perspectives and premises utterly at variance with Christian truth. His priorities have become subtly secularized. Thus, he can be emphatic about the evil of "sexual maladjustment" (pp. 35-44), but not about the evil of abortion. He concludes: "I have tried not to demand or plead in this book. But I would do either if it would discourage you from a medically unsafe abortion" (p. 95). Again, unsanitary surgical procedures are worth warning against; the application of "meat processing" techniques (McLuhan) to the unborn is not! Already the book has been commended as "open-ended" in the *Lutheran Women's Quarterly* (Fali, 1976, p. 24). Unsuspecting Christian women naturally trust that no deadly poison will be dispensed through church-related publications. The "open-ended" Weisheit books constitute in the deepest, biblical sense of that word, a *skandalon*. Good Lord, deliver us!

Christian News, December 27, 1976

1. Did LCMS President Jacob Preus do anything to stop CPH from publishing a pro-abortion book and a CPH sound filmstrip which denied justification by faith alone? ____.
2. Was action taken against Lutheran hospitals where unborn infants were being murdered? ____.
3. Rendering "no abortion except to prevent the mother's death" as "no abortion for any reason" indicates ____.
4. Modern knowledge corrects primitive folklore about ____.
5. It is a scientific fact that human life begins at ____.
6. The sight of babies and parts of babies in disposal bags outrages ____.
7. In 1973 the U.S. Supreme Court relaxed into pagan ____.
8. The controlling ideas of Weisheit's CPH published book simply do not represent ____.
9. What does the Oath of Hippocrates denounce? ____.
10. Almost all Clergy Counseling Service and Planned Parenthood groups are ____.
11. What has deeply infected the "counseling movement?" ____.
12. What did Solhenitsyn see eating at the vitals of civilization? ____.
13. What did the Lutheran Women's Quarterly say about the CPH book? ____.

KURT MARQUART ANSWERS
WAYNE SAFFEN

(Pastor Saffen's open letter to Pastor Marquart appeared in the December 23, 1974 C.N. Pastor Saffen is being defended by District President Paul Jacobs and ELIM. He was an LCMS chaplain at the University of Chicago and founded the Bonhoeffer House in Chicago. Pastor Marquart's letter deserves careful study. Ed.)

Dear Wayne:

If two professing Christians speaking the same language cannot communicate, this can only be, I put it to you, because either one or both of them do not want to.

All right, so I haven't the nicest desk side manner in the world. But if I can endure your abuse, ought not you likewise bear with my Kafkaesque eccentricities? I wouldn't dream of asking you to humor my paranoia for one moment—but what could be the harm in looking at a few public facts? And, honestly, I am getting better: I look for Brezhnev under my bed only once a fortnight now!

If by "authoritarians" you mean people who cultivate order in their intellectual lives, then I must say that it is only with such people that one can converse intelligently at all. But people whose ideas are plugged straight into their instincts, as it were, without solid ("authoritarian") underpinnings, cannot define anything coherently; hence conversation with them tends to go round and round in circles without getting anywhere. Thoughts, like cells, require structured integration into the total organism—they are not meant to flit dart and hither and yon like cancerous mavericks (cf Eph. 4:14).

And speaking of Ephesians (this time 6:17), what is wrong with "drawn swords?" Indeed I would even venture to say that a few neat, professional cuts with the sword are easier to take than heavy-handed bashings with plough shares!

At our annual Australian Lutheran students' conference last week we took a good look at Thomas Kuhn's *The Structure of Scientific Revolutions*. Kuhn stresses the crucial role of "paradigms" or theoretical frameworks for scientific activity and progress. It is there ordered conceptual models which give meaning and direction to research, i.e. "puzzle solving." If significant anomalies accumulate (that is, phenomena outside or counter to the expectations of the established paradigm), then the paradigm needs reconstruction or replacement, and a scientific revolution is on.

All this, it seems to me, is not without application to theological controversies. But of course one has to make allowances for the fact that science and theology have to be done in opposite directions, as it were. Science works toward truth as it terminates ad quem by straining the soup of reality through ever finer sieves, i.e. empirically/inductively controlled paradigms. Theology, on the other hand, has been given its Deposit of Faith once and for all, and must dip out the water of life from

78

this divinely revealed truth as its terminus a quo.

The information content of meaningful message in general is subject to corrosion at the hands of the Second Law of Thermodynamics (random "noise," misprints, etc.). In theology particularly this effect is heightened qualitatively by the ravages of sin, so that the whole history of theology is an ongoing crisis in the face of anti-Christian "cultural drifts," sometimes of tidal wave proportions. If the conflict is suppressed or disguised, pressures are built up towards the inevitable "theological revolution," e.g. the great paradigm-purification/restoration of the Reformation!

This is why it is so fatuous to imagine that the mere recitation of past formulas is sufficient "confession." On the contrary, it can be a rather shabby smokescreen to hide inability or refusal to construe, specify, and apply past confessions in relation to current issues and controversies. (See my *Affirm* piece on "Realism or Formalism in Theology").

To get down to tin tacks, it appears that your paradigm of the Missouri conflict is totally inadequate to cope with the reality. Your whole frame of reference is completely dominated, not to say obsessed, by secular/political imagery, Thus the historical-critical method makes sense to you not in terms of theological concepts and arguments, but only in the light of associations, conjured by the names of Kafka, McCarthy, Welch, Gary Allen (not *National Review* defector Garry Wills, whom you mistakenly named as author of "None Dare Call it Conspiracy"). Rockefeller, Agnew, Manion, and even poor Major Bundy, no doubt an imminent threat to America's civil libertines!

This dead-weight of irrelevance crushes all issues and forces you into unreasoning and ever shriller denunciations. (Has it not occurred to you, precisely from the standpoint of the grubby "realism" you affect, that power-motivated church-politicians are much more likely among smooth image-cultivators and consensus-mongers who never back the wrong horses and of whom all men speak well, than among stormy petrels prepared to devote time and energy to hopeless unfashionable treasures like Chemnitz's *The Two Natures in Christ?*) You do not even appear to notice the glaring contradiction between saying "God is Judge of all we do or say, not you or I," and then, a few lines later, "I will simply say that you do not know God. Nor does Preus or Otten or Werning, et. al.".! "*Thus Spake Saffen/Kafka*"!

Nor are you simply disdaining to argue, as you suggest. When you notice the slightest bit of promising material, you seize upon it quite eagerly, e.g. the Staubach quote. You even squeeze an argument out of two words by President Preus: "our theologians"! Yet despite such a sharp eye for subtleties, when it suits, you choose not to touch the historical-critical issue with one little finger, but rumble on about power politics instead. Why? Are you not courting that "fanatical spirit" which, says Luther, "stalks about like the car round the hot porridge, makes a terrible noise about our text and understanding not being right, but shies and flees like the devil before the Word of God, that he won't have to prove that his text and understanding are right; for he feels very well that he can't do it"? Adds Luther:

79

No that won't do. If you want to break down, then also build up. If you want to warn of error, then also teach the certain truth in its place, or else leave mastering and teaching alone. For thereby you admit your own defeat that you are a false, lying spirit, because you scold as false that the opposite of which you cannot and will not make true and certain. But the Holy Spirit knows very well how to prove and make certain the contrary, when He refutes lies of error (St. L. ed., XX, 902-903).

Your attempt to protect your total politicization onto me will not wash. I deplore and reject the Reformed confusion of the Two Kingdoms. And if you will read my discussion of "The Historical-Critical Method and Lutheran Presuppositions," shortly to be reprinted in America (don't know by whom yet), you will notice that it has nothing whatever to do with social or political considerations of any kind.

To my mind, historic Lutheran theology provides the ideal Christian paradigm of the nature and function of Holy Scripture. I have tried in my paper to sketch some of its salient features.

In my Open Letter to you I quoted the Keller book because it represents the historical-critical counter-paradigm with unusual honesty and clarity. In fairness you really ought to admit that this is not a "logical dodge" nor a "red herring," since I had already written a painstaking analysis ("The Swing of the Pendulum") for Affirm of your "beleaguered professors'" manifesto, "Faithful, etc." And ideas are today a global, ecumenical enterprise as never before. It is sheer obscurantism or worse to pretend that within the city limits of St. Louis, Missouri, the term "historical-critical method" might mean something unique and fundamentally different from what it means in the theological world at large!

One might even entertain such an improbable suggestion, had it been supported with rigorous definition and vigorous argumentation to show why the general understanding of the term was fallacious, and the St. Louis sense the valid and right one. But I have never heard of any attempt in this direction. The published theology was so fudged and flaccid as to the amount to a "non-paradigm"—except that the only alternative to paradigms are bad (i.e. woolly, evasive) paradigms!

If one is compelled then to adduce the Keller book as representing the gist of historical criticism, rather than the "beleaguered professors," this circumstance is not really a point in their favor. Indeed I am at a loss to know which is the more charitable assumption: that they could not or that they would not formulate more clearly.

From an objective, issue-oriented point of view at any rate it is evident that "Faithful, etc." represents neither historic Lutheran doctrine nor the consistent criticism of the Kellers, but an unstable, nebulous, transitional hybrid theology. It pays lip service to orthodoxy, yet re-interprets crucial terms to make room for the alien content of historical criticism, with its roots in the Enlightenment's triumphalism of human reason!

At least the Keller book makes no bones about this Enlightenment pedigree of the historical-critical method. If you are really resting your case, as you say, "with Jesus, throughout the Fourth Gospel," then you must repudiate a book which from beginning to end attacks precisely the

80

Jesus of the Fourth Gospel. Your refusal to do so shows that it is you who "cannot hear what the Kellers say."

Your non-theological, secular-political orientation emerges again when you accept the L.C.A. as "evangelical" because it allows Fortress Press to publish what it likes. Censorship would be "dictatorial". In other words, the term "evangelical" has become just another word for secular permissiveness. Just think for a moment what you are actually saying: Here is a book which blatantly denies that Jesus did any of the supernatural things attributed to Him in the Gospels, and reduces Him to "an ordinary man who did nothing like that at all." Yet publication of this anti-evangel you define as "evangelical," while refusal to do so would be "dictatorial" and therefore unevangelical! And then you want to rest your case "with Jesus, throughout the Fourth Gospel"!

The plain fact is that the Church has the duty to distinguish between Gospel and anti-Gospel, and to expose and attack all falsifications of the Gospel most energetically (Rom. 16:17; Gal. 1:6-9, etc.). The further fact is that the historical-critical method, by virtue of its origin and orientation, embodies the pseudo-gospel of our time, that is, the self-assertion of human reason over and against not only Biblical authority, but the Lordship of Christ and the very Incarnation itself.

This is the real curse of modern Christendom and constitutes what Prof. Peter Beyerhaus has called "the depth of the hermeneutical crisis in the WCC. There is no common conviction that the Bible is the authoritative and reliable basis for Christian faith and ministry. Scripture is seen by many as a collection of different historical documents..." (*Christianity Today,* March 30, 1973). The result is the total nihilism expressed by WCC Central Committee Chairman M. M. Thomas, at Bangkok:

> We are living at a time when we are deeply conscious of pluralism in the world—pluralism of human situations and needs, of varied religions and secular cultures, with different traditions of metaphysics, ideologies and world-views, in terms of which Christians themselves seek to express their commitment to and confession of Christ. So much so that any kind of a unity in the doctrine of Christ or of salvation in Christ, which has been the goal of traditional Christian churches, is to my mind impossible even of conception exception except in religious imperialistic terms. As a historian of religion, Wilfred Cantwell Smith, has recently said that on the grounds also of the loss of authority of the established churches today, "the old ideal of a unified or systematic Christian truth has gone. For this the ecumenical movement is too late," leaving a situation of "open variety, of optional alternatives," everyone choosing what suits him best (Questions of Religious Truth, pp. 34, 35).

Nor is this bankruptcy limited to a few people "at the top." The Greek Orthodox scholar Konstantinos E. Papaoetrou writes:

> The acute stage of the liberalization of theology is past, but on the other hand this liberalization has become chronic, deeper, more thorough. It has embraced wide circles of the church-people and the majority of the young West European pastors. "Demythologiz-

ing"...has for some time been more than a matter of a few academics; rather it largely shapes the consciousness of the Protestant churches... the whole of Christendom has embarked on a liberal course...the Protestant Christian today hears sermons which are possibly less liberal than some theological-scientific lectures at the turn of the century. But this subdued liberalism is no longer the content of lectures, but of sermons; it has even become self-evident (K.E. Papapetrou, "Ueber die anthropologischen Grenzen der Kirche" in *Arbeiten zur Geschichte und Theologie des Luthertums*, edited by W. Mauer, Karl H Rengstorf, E. Sommerlath, W. Zimmermann, vol. XXVI, p. 133).

It was the misfortune of the former St. Louis faculty majority that they allowed themselves to be used by those who felt it their right and duty to bring the Missouri Synod "up to date" by compromising with the historical-critical outlook prevailing in pan-Protestantism. And the Neo-Orthodox habit of evading substantive issues by choking all indicatives in a noxious fog of sanctimonious imperatives made it seem unnecessary to bother about precision, presuppositions, paradigms. (For classic sketch of a strikingly similar bout of well-intentioned theological abandon in French Roman Catholicism, see Etienne Gilson, *The Philosopher and Theology*, pp. 68 ff.). Hence the ultimate horrors implicit in the critical position were neither intended nor even perceived. Yet history is curiously indifferent to mere fond hopes and intentions and often produces objective effects and results quite at variance with them! I am sure, for instance, that there were devout and sincere Christians among the semi-Arians, who did not want a bar of Arian's blasphemies, but who had been talked into believing that "Athanasianism" was "extreme" and "sectarian" because it insisted on the new and unbiblical word "**homoouisious**." They thought that by rejecting the new word, they were simply retaining the old Christian confession!

The point is: The Missouri conflict is theological through and through, and is "political" only in the sense that churches with theological integrity must implement their confession in practice. Christian love will do everything possible to alleviate personal tragedies, but in principle it must be clear that the hearers' right to the uncorrupted life-giving truth of Christ takes precedence over any academic privileges or predilections of the church's public teachers.

I do not wish in any way to belittle the very real suffering endured by both sides, especially by the older men who have found themselves uprooted. But this suffering is only aggravated by triumphalist rhetoric which identifies an outward synodical structure with the Body of Christ in such a way that all theological issues must yield to the primacy of "togetherness" at any cost— even to the point of clinging to a synod one has pronounced dead and bankrupt! Missouri was founded on much more sober, Biblical, and limited notions of the nature and functions of visible church-bodies. The triumphalist, in his carnal eagerness to see the Body of Christ, fears "divisiveness" above all, and sacrifices theological integrity accordingly. Sober Lutheran ecclesiology, on the other hand, is content to believe the Body of Christ, while clinging to the pure Gospel and Sacraments of Christ's one Church, no matter what.

Furthermore, we comfortable Western Christians need to have our notions of suffering humbled a bit by relating them to world standards. The starving multitudes in Bangladesh would marvel at the great to-do made about a few men having to exchange one lot of luxurious jobs and homes for another lot, in institutions more in keeping with their ideas. To our Russian and Chinese colleagues, languishing in psychiatric torture chambers or slave labor camps, their wives and children reduced to paupers or worse, all the hardships of the "Seminex" dislocation must seem like Paradise itself!

And before you do another song and dance about my anti-communism, let me explain: One: I know next to nothing about the Church League of America, although they obviously got hold of some of my papers. Two: I try to be tolerant of all opinions within the spectrum of decency, but I am not attracted to maniacal types of "conservatism" which thinks (I have seen this in print) that Stalin's daughter, Svetlana, was a KGB plant!) Three: Love for our neighbor requires of us sobriety and realism in the civic realm. I can think of no better initiation into the realities of our time—as distinct from the fantasies of ideological cant and media-mania—than the magnificent autobiography of Malcolm Muggeridge and, for a Continental view. *Leftism* ("From de Sade and Marx to Hitler and Marcuse") by an Austrian nobleman with the magnificent name of Erik Maria Ritter von Kuehnelt-Leddihn (even though he is quite wrong about Luther)!

Should you choose to continue our exchange, please give top priority to theological clarification in general and to the historical-critical issue in particular.

Yours in our Epiphany King,
K. Marquart
Toowoomba, Australia

Christian News, January 27, 1975

1. Who was Wayne Saffen? ____.
2. Thoughts like cells require ____.
3. The whole history of theology is an ongoing ____.
4. If you want to warn of error then also teach ____.
5. Historic Lutheran theology provides the ideal Christian ____.
6. Faithful to our Calling-Faithful to our Lord of the liberal professors at Concordia Seminary has become another term for ____.
7. The term "evangelical" has become another term for ____.
8. The Church has the duty to distinguish between ____.
9. The historical critical method embodies ____.

Editor's Note: "Faithful to Our Calling – Faithful to Our Lord" by the Faculty of Concordia Seminary, St. Louis is in "Crisis in Christendom – Seminex Ablaze", pp. 131-142. "Unfaithful to Their Calling," Christian News, January 29, 1973 and "X-Raying the St. Louis Affirmations and Discussions" by Kurt Marquart, Christian News, April 9, 1973 are on pp. 126-130 of "Crisis in Christendom-Seminex Ablaze".

MARQUART LETTER
IN OCTOBER *REPORTER*

The Benke decision

Thank you for at least including Vice President Schulz's sobering remarks in your photo-celebration of the Benke victory (June, *Reporter*). The final decision may be a church-political triumph, but this is a theological fraud, resting on two bureaucratic untruths:

First, it is assumed that some loose language in a CTCR report covers the situation. In fact, the CTCR in its official response to the dispute-resolution panel stated that the section in question "does not explicitly address the issue of offering a prayer by an LCMS pastor in a 'civic event' in which prayers would also be offered by representatives of non-Christian religions."

Second, the Commission on Constitutional Matters invention that prior approval by an "ecclesiastical supervisor" in effect overrides Biblical and Confessional argumentation to the contrary, is an example of what Hermann Sasse has called the "institutional lie." He writes in "Union and Confession": "By this we mean a lie which works itself out in the institutions of the church, in her government and her organization. It is so dangerous because it legalizes the other lies in the church and makes them impossible to remove."

If the Yankee Stadium affair with official representatives of pagan religions was not a joint service, then there simply is no such thing. To pretend that all this is now happily behind us is to cry, "Peace, peace, when there is no peace" (Jer. 6:14; 8:11).

Prof. Kurt Marquart
Fort Wayne, Ind.

Christian News, October 6, 2003

1. What did Herman Sasse call the "Institutional lie?" ____.
2. If the Yankee Stadium affair with official representatives of pagan religions was not a joint service, then ____.

KIESCHNICK VS. MARQUART

For Such A Time As This: Marquart
for LCMS President

By: Al Schmidt

(Ed. Christian News is reprinting this article for all delegates to the LCMS's 2004 convention. Dr. Alvin Schmidt is a retired LCMS college and seminary professor and pastor. He is the author of several books including Under The Influence* and the Menace of Multiculturalism. Both are available from Christian News and are reviewed in this issue. CN is suggesting that the annual conference of the Association of Confessional Lutherans (p. 24) invites Dr. Jerry Kieschnick and Dr. Kurt Marquart, candidates for the presidency of the LCMS, to debate at the conference and then send a video of the debate to all delegates to the 2004 convention of the LCMS. Dr. Kieschnick and Dr. Marquart are among the top 5 nominees for LCMS President).

While some good confessional Lutheran candidates for the presidency of the Lutheran Church-Missouri Synod are being mentioned, I thought many in the LCMS, especially delegates to Synod's convention next summer might like to know why Kurt Marquart would be an excellent choice for Synod's president.

Having once been a colleague of his for a dozen years on the faculty of Concordia Theological Seminary in Fort Wayne, I have observed the following of his God-given gifts and talents:

1. He has a superb knowledge and command of God's Word, the Holy Scriptures.

2. He has an equally superb knowledge and command of the Lutheran Confessions.

3. He is a widely read person, one who also understands the impact of science, how it often influences theology, and how it often also shapes the thinking of many people.

4. He has the exceptional ability of using crisp, attention-getting words that illuminate problems often conflicting biblical concepts and Lutheran doctrine today.

5. His presentations are understood and admired in contexts outside of the church. For several years, Kurt and I were members of the Board of Directors of the Allen County Right to Life organization in Fort Wayne. This group had a lot of Catholic members, but when Kurt spoke, the people listened. Many times I heard them say "He surely knows how to discern the major issues." He was liked so well they even elected him as president of the organization.

6. He has published numerous biblically based, confessional Lutheran articles and books. They all underscore the great Lutheran teachings of *Solus Christus, Sola Gratia, Sola Fide, Sola Scriptura*, Law and Gospel,

as he applies them to problems of today in his gifted manner of speaking that is not staid or stodgy, a special talent already noted.

7. He does not speak from a theological ivory-tower. He is a layman's theologian.

8. He is excellent in apologetics, that is, he knows how to defend the Christian faith in an ever-increasing age of radical secularism and unbelief. Like St. Paul, he knows God put him here to defend the Gospel of Jesus Christ (Philippians 1:17). Just before Kurt joined the seminary faculty, I had introduced and taught the seminary's first course called "Modern Apologetics." Having been graduate dean at that time, I needed to lighten my teaching load, so when Kurt arrived from Australia, I suggested he should teach this course. He has been teaching it ever since. And many are the times I have heard former students of his (who are pastors now) say that they have learned more in this course, taught by Kurt than in most other courses.

9. He understands the nature of church bureaucracies and how they often short-circuit the mission of the church. Bureaucracies tend to alienate grass-root members, thereby stifling enthusiastic support, inducing financial commitment. He would bring a breath of fresh air to Synod's bureaucracy and reduce its pervasiveness.

10. He is known and respected internationally. He grew up in Europe before and during World War II; he speaks several languages; and he is highly regarded by confessional Lutherans in Australia, Eastern Europe, Haiti, Kenya, and Russia. For many years he served as a Lutheran pastor in Australia.

11. He has the ear of young people in the church. They like his clear and concise manner of speaking.

12. He has a wholesome sense of humor, a quality that would benefit all of us in Synod.

13. He speaks like a Lutheran, not like a generic Protestant. This helps Lutherans appreciate their heritage that is often camouflaged in our society's religiously syncretistic environment.

14. There is no guile in his mouth. When he disagrees with a statement or proposition, he does not attack the person with whom he disagrees. Even his opponents say this about him.

15. He has the heart of a spiritual shepherd, a genuine pastor, who knows when and how to use the Law, and when and how to use the Gospel.

16. His candidacy for the presidency of Synod, for which he has not volunteered, and about which I am sure he feels embarrassed, brings to mind the words Mordecai spoke to Esther: "Who knows whether you have not come to the kingdom for such a time as this?" (Esther 4:14).

Christian News, March 22, 2004

*Under the Influence is now titled *How Christianity Changed the World*.

1. Al Schmidt said that Kurt Marquart understands the impact of
____.
2. Marquart's articles and book all underscore ____.
3. Marquart is a ____ theologian.
4. Marquart taught ____ at Concordia Theological Seminary, Ft.
Wayne, Indiana.
5. Bureaucracies tend to ____.
6. Marquart has the heart of a ____.

KURT MARQUART FOR PRESIDENT

Dear Colleague in Ministry,

As most of us are aware, our church body is today facing perhaps one of the most challenging times in her history. Indeed, it may be spoken of as a time of crisis-crisis in doctrine and practice. Many are looking to the election of the synodical president next summer to be decisive in determining whether or not Missouri remains faithful to her historic, scriptural position in both confession and practice.

All of the confessional men that I have heard named as potential candidates for that office are faithful, devoted servants of the Word and the Church and would do a splendid job in maintaining an unashamedly Lutheran witness before the Church and the world.

But the substantive question is not whether one of these men is better in character than others. No. The real question before us, I believe, is simply: who among the confessional candidates is truly electable, especially against an incumbent who will have a well-oiled, well-funded, well-organized machine campaigning vigorously for him?

In other words, who among these has wide-spread name recognition within the Synod, is truly respected by all sides, does not enter the fray with negative baggage, has both national and international experience, and is possessed of impeccable credentials as a Lutheran theologian? Do we have someone to whom most everyone in the confessional camp would resonate as a leading candidate for Synodical President...and who would also widely appeal to those who are not comfortable with the current climate in the Synod, yet are undecided as to what to do about it? I believe we do have such a candidate!

I recently spoke with Professor Kurt Marquart and, because of recent news articles naming him as a potential candidate for president, asked him directly whether he would allow his name to be placed in nomination by congregations of the Synod, and if elected, would he serve. His answer was "yes" to both. He has no intentions of campaigning for office, but will do whatever the church asks him to do for her.

So why don't we ask him, through our nominations process and the election next summer, to be our next Synodical President! Does he possess the credentials? Yes. Would he possess the appeal to our Synod in convention that could unseat the incumbent and win the election? I believe he does. Would he provide the theological leadership and integrity Missouri so dearly needs -in her time of crisis? You answer that one.

Dear brother, I am writing to ask you to do three things: first of all, keep all this in your prayers before the throne of grace; second, if you yourself resonate to this proposal, offer Dr. Marquart's name to your congregation for nomination for Synodical President; and third, contact several more of our brothers in ministry who share our concerns and ask them to do the same.

May God bless you with strength to continue fighting the good fight of

the faith and may He bless the Missouri Synod in ways yet unseen!
Fraternally in Christ,
The Rev. Dr. John C. Stube,
Pastor
Ascension Lutheran Church & School
Fort Wayne, Indiana

Excerpt from an email
from Kurt Marquart

A student at the seminary took me on foot to his congregation where I was to preach. The trip took about three-quarters of an hour. The little church was made of clay walls and a tin roof with dirt floor. The altar area was slightly raised. Just before the service was to begin, the inevitable lizard dashed across the front of the altar. I preached about Peter attempting to walk on water, and said that in our baptism, we have so much more than just the ability to walk on water. During the offering (and I didn't have a single shilling left to put in the basket!), a father came to me and said his baby needed to be baptized. So we had a baptism, too. I wish I had not forgotten my camera, since it was an unforgettable experience. It is said that in a dark (poor) church, there are light hearts. And so it was.

Kurt in Africa

Supporters of Dr. Kurt Marquart for President are so very thankful to the organization that produced the "Crisis at the Crossroads" video and distributed it to every pastor in the LCMS . Although Kurt is more than happy to make this trip to Africa, many of us regret that he will not be available to visit our circuits and congregations to discuss the issues we face on a national church level.

That's right. For the entire winter quarter. Dr. Marquart will be teaching at the seminary in Motango, Kenya . . . a disappointing feat for students in this country who had signed on to take his classes. Nevertheless, Dr. Marquart departed January 3 to be of service to our brethren in Kenya, and we know that he will be a great encouragement and offer a rare period of total immersion for those students there.

Subjects Dr. Marquart will be teaching will include Modern Theology, Article III of the Augsburg Confession and Denominations-Symbolics. In a nation where sects are eager to gather up any and everyone, these valuable courses will be important tools for them in their defense of the Faith.

Christian News, March 29, 2004

JESUS FIRST RESPONDS TO CRISIS AT THE CROSSROADS VIDEO

The "tactics" Dr. Kurt Marquart "outlines - and displays - would actually work against Christ's mission" says the lead story in the February 2004 Jesus First. The story by Rev. Bruce A. Cameron is titled "A Response to the Marquart Campaign Video."

Christian News sent a copy of the video "Crisis At Crossroads - Summer 2004" to all of the some 6,000 congregations within the LCMS. However, many pastors, including both liberal and moderates supporting Dr. Jerry Kieschnick for president, and conservatives associated with some of the organized conservative groups within the LCMS, are not showing the video to their congregations. Twenty minutes of the video are excerpts of a speech Marquart presented at the Walther Conference held at Concordia Seminary, St. Louis on November 7 and 8 and answers to questions he was asked by a reporter after the conference. Fifty minutes of the video show what actually happened at Yankee Stadium on September 23, 2001 when Dr. David Benke with Kieschnick's permission prayed with Muslims, Sikhs, Jews, Buddhists and others.

LCMS liberals, like those associated with Jesus First and DayStar, do not appreciate Marquart's defense of the LCMS scriptural and confessional position on the inerrancy of the Bible, evolution and creation, the ordination of women, abortion and homosexuality. The LCMS liberals supporting Dr. Jerry Kieschnick for LCMS president want a president who will not support any disciplinary action against those on the LCMS clergy roster who maintain that the LCMS should be broad enough to include pastors and teachers who promote the ordination of women, deny the inerrancy of the Bible, maintain that evolution is a fact, and who insist that it is permissible to be in fellowship with those who support abortion and homosexual pastors.

Marquart has been teaching in Kenya during the last eight weeks. Marquart, who speaks several languages, has taught pastors in various nations, throughout the world, including Russia.

Throughout his ministry, besides speaking and teaching several languages in many nations, Marquart has generously supported mission work. He has often used his own funds to support native pastors and students in poor nations rather than using this money for himself and a costly home. The liberals, who complain Marquart's "tactics" work against Christ's mission have never complained about the lavish life style of Dr. Jerry Kieschnick and his more than a half million dollar home he purchased in St. Louis when he became president of the LCMS. They have not protested that Kieschnick insists that the LCMS pay for the traveling expenses of his wife who often accompanies him on his many

90

flights throughout the U.S. and overseas.

While Marquart has his sharp critics on the left, the organized "right" is also not supporting him. So far the "Crisis at the Crossroads - Summer 2004" video has not been mentioned in any of the many conservative publications and web sites in the LCMS other than Pastor Jack Cascione's Reclaim News. Many of the organized conservatives do not appreciate Marquart's support the rights of laymen and defense of the position of Dr. C.F.W. Walther on Church and Ministry reaffirmed at the LCMS's 2001 convention. Some of organized conservatives who refuse to promote Marquart and even show the video featuring Marquart to their congregations, prefer the Episcopal position promoted by such Lutheran theologians as Loehe, Grabau and Stephan. One prominent LCMS leader has referred to this group as almost "a cult." Marquart is the candidate preferred by the "center" party in the LCMS, the "grassroots " conservatives who promote the scriptural and confessional position the LCMS has always taught. They say they are neither at the "Left" nor the "Right" but at the "Center" of the LCMS's historic scriptural position.

Many on the "right" who are not nominating Marquart are among those who opposed the LCMS's 2001 convention resolution reaffirming the historical position of the LCMS. They are urging congregations to nominate Concordia Seminary, Ft. Wayne President Dean Wenthe.

"A Response to the Marquart Campaign Video" in the February, 2004 Jesus First said:

A RESPONSE TO THE MARQUART CAMPAIGN VIDEO
By Bruce A. Cameron

The Kurt Marquart campaign video arrived at every LCMS congregation along with the Christmas mail. Marquart, a professor at Concordia Theological Seminary, Ft. Wayne, Indiana, says that the LCMS will reach a "crisis at the crossroads" at the July 2004 synodical convention. The video spells out Professor Marquart's platform, expressly encouraging congregations to nominate him for President of the LCMS.

Marquart's Crisis

Professor Marquart says that the LCMS "needs to decide at this convention whether the Synod seriously wishes to remain a confessional Lutheran church." Central to this crisis diagnosis is "the crass syncretism in New York" and the subsequent "public whitewash of a notorious case of syncretism."

Marquart is referring to LCMS Atlantic District President Dr. David Benke's Christian prayer in a public event that included other religions at Yankee Stadium following September 11, 2001. Marquart and others believe that, by praying, Benke was declaring unity of belief with Hindus, Muslims and Jews and should recant his participation or else be expelled from the LCMS. The vast majority of LCMS members, myself included, do not agree that Benke was declaring unity of belief with them (nor they with us). The massive outpouring of support for President Benke (and for synodical President Gerald Kieschnick who approved Benke's participation) testifies that most LCMS members do not agree with Marquart's crisis diagnosis.

Is Bureaucracy the Culprit?

Professor Marquart sees nothing but "bureaucratic maneuvering" in Benke's vindication of charges brought against him, indicating a "bureaucratic spirit in our church that cannot put the issue of truth first."

What Marquart fails to mention is that Benke's accusers chose to attack him on the basis of the Bylaws and Constitution of the LCMS. That the accusers, including Marquart, should afterwards be "Shocked! Shocked!" that the synodical panel hearing the accusations based its decisions on the Bylaws and Constitution of the LCMS ["purely organizational bureaucratic trivia"] seems less than believable. The congregations of our Synod have formed structures, constitutions and bylaws to serve our synodical goals, a fact that Marquart himself acknowledges. One who is running for the office of administrator of a "bureaucracy" should be wary of bad-mouthing the existence of that bureaucracy.

Marquart's Solution

The video continues with a clear picture of a Marquart presidency:

It is "essential to discontinue any joint church or chaplaincy work with the ELCA," says Marquart. Should nursing home and hospital ministries where congregations of both church bodies support a single chaplain be discontinued? Local congregations, not a top-down mandate, could better decide.

The Synod "needs to reassert effective doctrinal discipline within its Concordia University System" where, Marquart says, the "old Seminex theology is . . . rising again to haunt us." Really? I hear a different concern from lay people.

Professor Marquart addresses our Synod's understanding of "the nature of the Gospel ministry," opposing both "lay ministry" and "exaggerated clericalism." I see the latter is a real problem.

We need to address the "open scandal" of the "continued existence of neo-Pentecostalism in our Synod," he asserts. Where is that?, I ask.

"Let the decisions of the Commission on Constitutional Matters (CCM) be advisory," he advises. Should we really remove the only process we have to resolve questions and disputes between conventions?

Marquart proposes a "return to a proper adjudication and appeal system interested in pursuing and asserting the divine truth rather than simply sorting out personal conflicts by means of mediation, arbitration and compromise–important as that can be at times." During the era of the earlier system, based on an adversarial model, synodical entities actually advised turning to the civil courts. We should be very hesitant to ditch the Reconciliation Process that has blessed our Synod.

I cannot support Professor Marquart's platform. While I am sure we are united on our objective–to bring the one message of Jesus Christ to as many people as possible–he does not articulate a clear strategy to further this objective. And the tactics he outlines–and displays–would actually work against Christ's mission.

Rev. Bruce A. Cameron is pastor of St. John Lutheran Church, Sparta, IL.

Christian News, March 1, 2004

1. The video "Crisis at the Crossroads-Summer 2004" included ____.
2. Marquart who speaks ____ languages has taught pastors in ____.
3. Why did many of the organized conservatives not support him for LCMS president.

THE QUESTION OF PROCEDURE
IN THEOLOGICAL CONTROVERSIES

From the April-September, 1966
Australasian Theological Review

Kurt Marquart

This paper does not pretend to be anything like a systematic treatment of some such *locus* of Moral Theology as *"De Controversiis."* Nor is it intended as an assortment of conceivable *casualia,* or as an attempt to construct Canon Law from precedents. The object is, rather, to treat certain fundamental principles, and to do so with special reference to (1) the democratic, congregational type of church polity with which we are familiar, and (2) genuine, serious theological controversies, rather than mere silly squabbles or purely local agitations.

I. Truth and Love

It would appear that theological controversies cannot proceed very far before charges of "lovelessness" are raised by one or the other side. It behooves us therefore to examine the relevance and validity of such charges.

It is clear that even the best of Christians daily violate love. i.e. fall short of perfect charity. It is equally obvious that any sort of controversy will tend to excite not only righteous wrath, but also a whole clan of its less noble, carnal cousins! Since this failing would, presumably, be the common property of both sides of any dispute, it is difficult to see how it could be exploited by the partisans of one side! And it is safe to predict that not many will want to assume a sort of divine comedy, or miracle-in-reverse, whereby false doctrine becomes a guarantee of immunity from the propensities of the flesh, so that, given a dispute between the adherents of true and false doctrine respectively, only the former suffer from the malaise of lovelessness, while the latter are veritable Knights of Charity.

Obviously it cannot be this sort of thing which is meant by charges of "lovelessness." The real target of the attack seems to be that unbending adamance which is characteristic of the confessional attitude. For genuine Biblical commitment, broad, secular "reasonableness" has neither understanding nor tolerance. The ire of the world and of worldly churchmen is aroused not so much by the divine truth itself—that, after all, could be accommodated somehow in the pantheon of "views"—as by the inconvenient determination of its confessors to take that truth seriously, to live and die by it. Dr. C. F. W. Walther put it this way:

> "It has always been not so much the pure doctrine *per se,* which has aroused hostility against its representatives, much less is that the case in our indifferent age, but taking it seriously, the exclusive adherence to it, the rejection and condemnation of the opposite doc-

trine, and above all the practical implementation of this doctrinal position, that is was "which at all times provoked hostility... So also the Cardinal of Salzburg said that Luther's doctrine 'he would tolerate, but to allow oneself to be reformed out of a corner (aus dem Winkel), that was not to be tolerated.' So it still is today. What doctrine isn't one prepared to tolerate nowadays, if only it will stand peacefully beside the other doctrine! And just those who want to be orthodox accomplish the most incredible fears in this tolerance. Only observe the harmonious relation, which shows itself in the academic colleges, the peaceable sitting together in pastoral conferences, the tone in the reviews!" (*Lehre und Wehre,* Jan. 1879, p. 1).

The world's love is a curious amalgam of sentimentality, callousness, and expediency. How different from Biblical *agape!* Ibsen put these flaming words into the mouth of Pastor Brand: "What the world calls love I neither know nor want. I know God's love, and that is not weak and mild. That is hard even unto the terror of death; it offers caresses which leave wounds" (Brand, condensed by Dorothy Hoyer Scharlemann, Act III). True, Biblical love is always dominated from above. It throws with the crimson of fire and of blood, and has no kinship whatever to the fraudulent pastels of sentimental philanthropy or egalitarian humanitarianism—and their religious counterpart: unionism. Only God may be loved absolutely. The First Table of the Law precedes and determines the Second, as the First Commandment precedes and determines all the others. When this anchorage in God is given up, and the Second Table, or love of Man, is absolutized, then God is no longer love; instead. Love is god! Such "love" is but an egalitarian, relativistic quicksand, which swallows up all distinctions between truth and error, right and wrong. But when objective standards and norms are gone, and the principle, *quod licet Jovi non licet bovi* (what is permissible for Jove is not permissible for an ox), is no longer intelligible, much less workable, such an oozing, undifferentiated "love" easily and quickly becomes an oppressive paternalism, i.e. tyranny. George Orwell, in describing the nightmarish police-state of *1984,* adds a masterly touch when he has the horrible, heavily armed "law" enforcement agency called, officially, the "Ministry of Love"!

There is an important sense in which I must love Unitarians and Communists. But this does not mean that I have the right, much less the duty, to admit them into my pulpit. Love and ecclesiastical recognition are neither synonymous nor coextensive. No Christian churchman should dream of complaining when Truth is given precedence over Love, or, more accurately, love for God and His Word over love for man. This relationship is elementary in the Kingdom of God. "Pure love to the individual has its roots in the love to God, love to the disciple in love to the Master, love to the member in love to the Church, and the broader love must be the determiner of and controlling force to the narrower" (C. P. Krauth, quoted in S.E. Ochsenford, *Doctrinal History of the General Council of the Lutheran Church in North America).*

Luther asserts, in his typically blunt way, the supremacy of Truth over Love in countless passages. Here are a few examples:

"Faith and love are two different things. Faith tolerates nothing, love tolerates everything; faith curses, love blesses; faith seeks revenge and punishment, love seeks to spare and to forgive. Therefore, when faith and God's Word are involved, there can be no more loving or being patient, but only anger, zeal, and scolding. All prophets also acted in this way, that in matters of faith they showed no patience or mercy." (St. Louis ed., V, 38).

"Therefore in mere ceremonies love shall be judge and mistress, but not in matters of faith or of the promises of God. . . . Rather, faith shall be lord over love, and to it love shall yield, but faith shall not yield to love" (Theses against the Council of Constance. 1535).

"Nothing must be allowed to harm God and His Word. This must take precedence over everything else. All things must be sacrificed for it. Here we must give consideration neither to friend or foe. For this is something that does not belong to us, nor to the neighbor, but to God Himself . . . . Therefore I say to my most bitter enemies:
. . . Since you do not want to submit to that Word, I will speak this prayer and blessing over you. May God hinder you and bring you to shame! I will gladly serve you, but not when you want to overthrow God's Word. Here you will not prevail upon me to give you one drink of water. . . .The Bible says. Thou shalt love thine enemy and do good to him. But I must be an enemy of God's enemies, lest I attack God with them" (VII, 481).

"There are two kinds of sins, the first against the Word, or the Christian doctrine and creed; the other, against love. Sin against the doctrine should in no way be tolerated. But with the sin against love, we should have patience, for in such a sin one acts against the neighbor without any harm to the doctrine or the creed. But where something is done against the Word, the creed, and God's Honor, there one should under no circumstances remain silent, there must be far less patience, and one must oppose it vigorously" (XIX, 1182).

In a day when saccharine "devotional" booklets have displaced the Psalter in the spiritual life of even many orthodox Christians, it is not to be expected that Luther's rugged language will find wide acceptance. Yet this ruggedness was one of Luther's most Christ-like traits! Consider Dr. M. Franzmann's eloquent reminder:

"Where the Christ is proclaimed, there will always be both, confessors and deniers, for . . . . the Christ is the Christ who sunders and divides. . . . The Messiah is the Prince of Peace . . . But He brings no cheap peace, half peace, no peace by compromise. He can create peace only by destroying evil; and since men love evil and cling to that which excludes them from the whole peace of God, His coming forces a decision between good and evil and proves to be, for all its peaceful intent, the sundering sword. . . .
The division cuts through all human connections and dissolves every nexus that human life knows. And since it is an absolute division, the decision and the renunciation which it involves are agonizingly absolute. . . .

96

This is no soft and mellow Jesus, no pink-and-blue Christ; there is no such Jesus Christ in our records of Him. And these apostles are not suavely robed young suavely robed young saints looking beatific against a bright Italian sky" (*Follow Me*, p. 96).

Since our Lord Himself, Perfect Love Incarnate, on occasion acted in ways (cleansing the Temple, for example) which did not, on the surface, make the presence of love apparent, it is clear that genuine, God-pleasing love cannot simply be judged by general outward appearances, such as someone's experience of embarrassment, unpleasantness, or even acute distress. True love may appear outwardly to be *its* opposite, while seeming love may turn out to be that false kind which Luther rightly calls "accursed." Love cannot be converted into a brittle code of external regulations!

It was no doubt for this reason that Dr. F. Pieper penned these wise words:

"The *principle* all Christians must acknowledge . . . But not in every *particular* case may one command a Christian that he must practice love, and much less, in what *measure* that must happen. That one must leave to Christian judgment" (*Vortraege*, p. 120).

In the final analysis love is a mystery of the heart, over which God has not appointed human judges (St. Mat. 7:1). *De occultis non judicat ecclesia.* Only in those relatively rare cases when Scripturally defined external criteria have been breached demonstrably, should a charge of lovelessness be levelled, lest the charge itself be more loveless than the act condemned.

It is clear that in the context of a genuine theological controversy the charge of "lovelessness" is singularly inept, and should never be raised in isolation from the substantive question *of* the truth or falsehood of the doctrines debated. History teaches us to suspect that he who bases his case mainly on appeals to love, unity, etc., is trying to dodge an issue. Attention should be focused on the objective doctrinal issues, not on the entrails of the participants, which are irrelevant in this connection. After all, when someone claims that there is a bomb aboard an airplane, it is the verification of this allegation, and not the caller's state of mind that is of urgent, immediate, and primary interest.

To conclude this section, here are two quotes, one from Dr. C. F.W. Walther, and the other from a 1935 *Lutheran Witness* editorial:

"Never has there been so much talk about 'love' as in our day. 'Love' has become the slogan and watchword of those who claim to be Christians as well as those who do not care to be called Christians. Now what do such Christians mean when they speak about 'love'? They mean, above all, as they express it, that in matters of faith one must exhibit tolerance, that is, endurance, indulgence, and the spirit of compromise: that one must not be so exact in regard to purity of doctrine, nor criticize the departure from the Word of God as strenuously as was done in olden times; and that we ought, therefore, also recognize those as brethren who are not willing to obey the Word of God in some points, as long as they accept a few espe-

97

cially important articles of faith. But how? Should that really be a true description of Christian 'love'? Does not the Word of God say the very opposite: 'Charity rejoiceth not in iniquity but rejoiceth in the truth'? (I Cor. 13:6). Such Christians (who out of 'love' tolerate false doctrine) are like the man who was very liberal and charitable toward the poor. What he gave them, however, he did not take from his own goods, but what he had secretly stolen from others. That he openly gave to the poor. For what are those Christians doing but robbing God of His Word, His Truth, His Glory, and thereby giving the impression that they have more love than others (who adhere strictly to God's Word)? Just how little 'love' such people really possess may be seen by their attitude toward those who take them to task for their indifference to the Truth. Against such (true disciples, John 8:13ff), they are mostly filled with rancor, venom, and bitter enmity" (*Hausandachten,* p. 92, quoted in *Lutheran Loyalty,* July, 1951).

"During the Spanish-American War unscrupulous greed led certain men to sell tainted meat; many of our soldiers became ill, suffered torture and a great number died. The culprits were exposed and punished. Was it lack of charity to expose them and to hand them over to justice?

. . . A gang of robbers had carefully planned an armed robbery of one of the banks. They were a notorious band. A few murders did not seem to mean anything to them. By devious ways somebody learned the plot. He exposed it to the authorities. Because of that exposure some of the robbers are dead, while the others are in prison. Was it lack of charity to expose the plot? . . .

Is it lack of charity to warn against false doctrine? There are some who will most emphatically reply in the affirmative. . . . Is it an act of charity for a child of God to remain silent in order to spare the feelings of people with good intentions?

If that be charity, our Savior was most uncharitable. . . . The same thing applies to all the apostles. . . . God Himself makes it the duty of His children to contend for His honor. For those who fail Him in this He has words of the severest condemnation, calling them 'dumb dogs.' . . . swayed by the ungodly spirit of unionism, some would not only remain silent themselves, but expect silence on the part of ethers lest somebody be offended. . . . May God give us true charity!" (L.W.Nov. 5, 1935).

II. The Eighth Commandment and St. Matthew 18

There is a certain pietistic tendency to blunt and smother confessional impulses with "the Law of Love." No one will deny that the phrase has some meaningful and important uses. It may even happen that pastors or church officials and committees feel constrained to administer public rebukes in the name of the Law of Love. But one thing that should not be done with the phrase is to make it the basis of disciplinary proceedings. For that function the expression, by itself, in isolation from other more specific Scriptural injunctions, is entirely too vague and broad. For disciplinary purposes there is no abstract "Law of Love" floating above and beyond all specific commands and prohibitions. Such a construct is dangerously arbitrary and infringes upon the responsible, legitimate freedom of Christian conscience. Devoid of concrete, Scripturally verifiable content can serve only to tyrannize consciences through the imposition of someone's personal, arbitrary judgments and/or prejudices. As no secular court would accept and act upon a charge of "violation of the law of the land," without reference to a specific statute alleged to have been broken, so the Church should not countenance any disciplinary action on the basis of a conveniently ethereal "Law of Love."

The usual purpose of such references to the "Law of Love" is the protection of the reputation and honor of embattled theologians. But this purpose is served much better by referring to the Eighth Commandment, which represents, concretely and specifically, the Law of Love at that particular point. And the procedure of admonition given by the Lord in St. Mat. 18 may be regarded, in this connection, as a subsidiary provision of the Eighth Commandment.

The question now arises whether and to what extent theologians involved in controversy may claim protection for themselves and their utterances under the Eighth Commandment. Without entering upon the details of casuistry, it is safe to offer three generalizations:

1. Error has no rights in the Church. With respect to doctrine the Christian Church is not a republic, in which all views enjoy equal rights, but an absolute monarchy, in which all subjects are irrevocably committed to the Word of their divine King, as promulgated in His Prophetic-Apostolic Constitution. Luther writes, in his comments on the 82nd Psalm:

"We read that the holy Fathers at the Nicene Council, as soon as they heard the Arians' doctrine read, hissed unanimously (*zischten sie alle eintraeschtiglich*) and would not hear it, nor let it be demonstrated or defended, but condemned them forthwith without any debating, as public blasphemers. Moses in his Law also commands to stone such blasphemers, indeed all false blasphemers. So also here one should not make much disputing but condemn such public blasphemy even without a hearing and defense (*unverhoert und unverantworter*); as also St. Paul commands in Tit. 3, that a heretic is to be avoided, when he has been admonished once or twice; and he forbids Timothy logomachy and disputing, which does nothing but pervert the hearers. For such universal article of all of Christendom have already been sufficiently examined, proved, and decided through the holy Scripture and the confession of the whole of universal Christendom, confirmed with many miraculous signs, sealed with much blood of the holy martyrs, witnessed and defended in the books of all teachers, and need no more mastering and probing *(Kluegeln)*" (Porra, *Pastorale Lutheri,* 577-8).

Needless to say, this does not mean that hitherto Orthodox theologians may be condemned without a conclusive demonstration that they have in fact fallen into heresy.

2. Public doctrinal error normally requires public correction, and by no means always necessitates previous personal dealings. Likewise, secret doctrinal error may and must be revealed, with or without personal dealings if the Church's doctrinal integrity is threatened. "I spake openly to the world: I ever taught in the synagogue, and in the temple whither the Jews always resort; and in secret have I said nothing. *Why askest thou Me? Ask them which heard Me,* what I have said unto them: behold, they know what I said" (St. John 18:20,21).

"Them that sin rebuke before all, that others also may fear" (I Tim. 5:20).

St. Paul issued specific rebukes On the basis of the testimony of others:

I Cor. 1:11: "It hath been declared to me of you..."
I Cor. 5:1: "It is reported commonly..."
I Cor. 11:17; "I hear that..."
I Cor. 15:12: "How say some among you..."
II Thess. 3:11: "We hear that there are some..."
Cf. also Gal. 1:6 and 4:10 ff.. which record rebukes written, evidently, on the strength of witnesses' reports.

The Large Catechism says:

"All this has been said regarding secret sins. But where the sin is quite public, so that the judge and everybody know it, you can without any sin avoid him and let him go, because he has brought himself into disgrace, and you may also publicly testify concerning him. For when a matter is public in the light of day, there can be no slandering or false judging or testifying; as when we now reprove the Pope with his doctrine, which is publicly set forth in books and proclaimed in all the world. For where the sin is public, the reproof also must be public, that everyone may learn to guard against it" (8th Commandment, par. 284).

That the various stages of Matt. 18 need not apply to public sins, is an accepted principle of Pastoral Theology:

"Whenever the committing of a sin has become generally known and public offense has been given, it is not necessary to observe the three degrees of admonition prescribed in Matt. 18" (Fritz, *Past. Th.* 232).

Very interesting is Luther's statement in his Reply at Worms:

"The third kind consists of those books which I have written against private individuals, so-called, against those, that is, who have exerted themselves in defense of the Roman tyranny and to the overthrow of that piety which I have taught. I confess that I have been more harsh against them than befits my religious vows and my profession. For I do not make myself out to be any kind of saint, nor am I now contending about my conduct but about Christian doctrine. But it is not in my power to recant them, because that recantation would give that tyranny and blasphemy an occasion to lord it over those whom I defend and to rage against God's people more violently than ever" (Bettenson, *Documents of the Christian Church,* 2nd ed., pp. 281-282).

Sometimes a situation arises in the Church which can only be described as conspiratorial. That happened, for example, at the University of Wittenberg after Luther's death, when the Crypto-Calvinists nearly succeeded in destroying the Lutheran Church from within. One of the conspirators, Peucer, wrote a letter to his friend Christian Schuetze, a crypto Calvinistic court-preacher in Dresden. By mistake, or rather by God's gracious direction, as Dr. Walther observes (*Concordienformel,* p. 54), the letter fell into the hands of another, orthodox, court preacher, Lysthen, who promptly transmitted the incriminatory document to the rather naive Elector August, thus at last opening his eyes to the conspiracy. Lengthy private dealings with the conspirators, and perhaps a gentlemanly gesture, such as returning the letter, would clearly have harmed the Church, and were therefore out of place.

The following instructive opinions were considered important enough to be included by Dedeken in his formidable compilation which bears the even more formidable official title: '*Thesaurus consiliorum et decisionum, d. i. vornehmer Universitaeten, hochloeblicher Collegien, Consistorien auch sonst hochgelehrter Theologen und Juristen Rath, Bedenken, Antwort, Belehrung, Erkenntnis, Bescheid und Urtheil in und von allerhand schweren Faellen, in Druck gegeben durch M. Georg Dedekennum.* Hamburg, 1623."

In Vol. 1, pp. 864-865, an opinion by the ministerium of Riga is given regarding the question whether public sin must first be verified before being rebuked. This is vigorously denied, with the argumentation that John the Baptist did not ask Herod what he had done (he might have denied it), but condemned his public sin, as also Nathan did with David.

In Vol. II, p. 296, we have, beside a citation of Scripture's approval of spying for a good cause (as in the land of Canaan), the following opinion by Luther:

> "Whether sin and evil, or else secret things from which evil is to be feared, may be reported by a good Christian to the spiritual or temporal authority, according to the nature of the matter, or whether that is to be considered a betrayal? . . . it is no sin, but praiseworthy, when known and offensive sin and evil deed, or secret things from which evil can come, are brought before those before whom it belongs, such as authorities, spiritual and temporal, parents and teachers and the like. . . . Thus Joseph brought before his father that there was an evil rumor against his brothers, Gen. 37:2. To David it was reported that everyone's heart followed Absalom, and what other designs he had against his father, II Sam. 15 and 17. Mordecai brought before King Ahasuerus that two chamberlains sought to lay hands upon the king, Esther 2:22. Saint Paul's sister's son brought the conspiracy which some Jews had made against him, before St. Paul, and through him to the captain; thereby Paul's life was saved. Acts 23;16ff.

"Such revelations of secret evil designs and deeds, whereby great damage can be prevented, are a piece of Christian love. . . . Therefore one may not regard it as betrayal. . . ."

And only last year the Texas District (Missouri Synod) Board of Appeals rendered an extremely significant decision (Texas District Praesidium vs. Pastor Francis Machina) which asserts:

"It is our judgment that the defendant has produced sufficient proof to sustain the position that personal confrontation is not always necessary, not even with respect to Matt. 18, when the matter is public. Authorities citied are Scripture, *Walther's Pastorale,* Fritz' *Pastoral Theology,* Luther's *Large Catechism,* and authorities in Synod.

"Therefore it is our opinion that an offended brother may well publicly attack a public matter without personal confrontation."

3. This does not mean that contentious, censorious individuals are free to snatch up casual remarks of otherwise orthodox teachers and forthwith to broadcast them, together with invidious interpretations. Misunderstandings can easily occur, and even when some casual aberration of an otherwise orthodox theologian is real, genuine fraternal consultation offers the greatest hope of success.

The undersigned is convinced that some of the violent theological convulsions overseas are traceable, in part, to a certain unimaginative smugness in the past, coupled with an extreme and myopic brittleness and fussiness which fails to distinguish between divine truth and mere ecclesiastical tradition, the divine content and the particular historical form (though these terms are horribly abused nowadays). *Speaking the Truth in Love,* although designed to promote a disastrous theological fallacy regarding Church Fellowship, nevertheless contains at least one very valid paragraph:

"When the *Lutheran Witness,* in 1931, complimented a congregation on making its quota for Synod, a conference took note of the fact that this congregation had no parish school and that therefore 'the entire tone and scope of said article is out of line with Synod's accepted principles.' The conference asked the *Witness* to make proper explanations. From the editorial reply, 'I notice a growing tendency to elevate certain time-honored attitudes to the rank of principles, and then to make these principles serve almost as tests of good Missourianism or even of Lutheranism. I look with some alarm at such a free use of the term "Synod's accepted principles" as it occurs in your letter. I would caution against using such a line of argument whenever something has been done that displeases a brother. I would, of course, not take notice of this phrase, if I had not seen some very sincere and also intelligent brethren suffer reproach because of some deduction that was made which involved him in conflict, with the "standards of our Synod." The more of these yokes we hang upon the brethren, the more we shall produce a reaction of liberalism and radicalism. . . . There must be utter freedom of expression and action, all governed by the principle of love, wherever the Word of God has not spoken the decisive word'."

Orthodoxy, far from being narrow, sterile, dead, etc., actually possesses a vast and thrilling catholicity of perspective, whose breathtaking grandeur dwarfs the tiny, confining superficialities of the ephemeral *isms!* We do the Church and her orthodox Faith a distinct disservice when we act as though the divine truth may be uttered only in one stereotyped way, and must be compressed into only one mold of devotion. The gifts of the Spirit are many and varied, but they all exist to edify the one Body. We must not be afraid of a healthy variety of expression—the New Testament itself is the best example of the strikingly different ways in which the one Gospel can be put—even while we jealously guard the continuing identity of our proclamation with the Apostolic, Biblical *depositum fidei* and with the unbroken teaching tradition of the orthodox Church.

Christian News, November 28, 1966

Editor's Note: "Praesidium of the Texas District vs. Francis Machina – Opinion of the Board of Appeals of the Texas District The Lutheran Church-Missouri Synod was published in the August 26, 1963 *Christian News* and *A Christian Handbook on Vital Issues*, pp. 738-739. Marquart was Machina's first counselor in this case. Herman Otten took Marquart's place when he was called to Australia. Otten was the counselor and also a witness when the case was heard in Austin, Texas. Texas District officials at first refused to answer Otten's questions. The Board of Appeals ordered them to answer.

1. Theological controversies cannot proceed very far before charges of ____ are raised.
2. What did the Cardinal of Salzburg say? ____.
3. What did Ibsen put into the mouth of Pastor Brand? ____.
4. No Christian churchman should dream of complaining when Truth is given precedence over ____.
5. Luther recognized the supremacy of ____ over love.
6. Error has no rights in the ____.
7. Public doctrinal error normally requires ____.
8. Jesus said that in ____ I have said nothing.
9. Where the sin is public the reproof must also be ____.
10. What did the LCMS's Texas District Board of Appeals rule in the Machina Case about Matthew 18? ____.
11. We must not be afraid of a healthy variety of ____.

GRAVE MISGIVINGS – WOMAN'S SUFFRAGE IN THE CHURCH

Without sharing all your judgments and approaches, I thoroughly respect your confessional integrity, and therefore consider that the continuation of a Liberal regime's self-serving vendetta against you is unjust and offensive. It is for this very reason that I am duty-bound to express grave misgivings about the July 2 issue of Christian News.

It goes without saying that I oppose the malicious rumor-mongering against President Robert Preus of our Seminary. But in order to defend him against these unfounded insinuations it is not necessary to subject the Synod's President to the same sort of personal attacks as those rightly complained of in the case of Dr. Preus.

Unless we (and I include myself) rigorously discipline our rhetoric, we shall damage the very framework within which current differences can and must be resolved, calmly and fraternally. That framework includes a maintenance of such courtesy towards the church's responsible officials as our respect for the church itself demands. Disagreements may be unavoidable, but insults are not. I urge and beg you not to inflame an already volatile situation further.

There are indeed grave theological issues before our Lutheran church in this country, but the "doctrine" (?!) of women' s suffrage is not one of them. The merging Lutheran churches are, through their dialogue committees, negotiating away the very presence of Christ's holy body and blood in the Sacrament of the Altar—and who even notices it or cares? Contrary to the whole Book of Concord the Lutheran-Reformed Dialogue maintains the blatant untruth that the Reformed churches "have always taught and still teach the real presence of Christ in the Eucharist" (An Invitation to Action, Fortress, 1984, p. 114), and that they differ with us only over the "mode" of this presence! See Formula of Concord, S.D., VII, 1-7, for a description of the very same tricks of language which were then unanimously rejected by our church, but are now palmed off on confessionally drowsy Lutherans as the "real presence."

Within our own Synod an urgent problem is the re-appropriation of our confessional heritage in the matter of church and ministry. To this extent at least Brother Clyde Nehrenz is right (*Christian News*, June 25). But his article is long on vehemence and short on argument. Obviously I cannot take up the whole thing here, but let me give three simple facts which do not fit Mr. Nehrenz's "model." The latter indeed reflects views held in Missouri's "bronze age," but is quite inadequate as a representation of our historic position and understanding.

The three facts are: (1) in Luther's time (1535) the Prince Elector of Saxony authorized the Wittenberg theological faculty to administer Ordination for his entire realm. (2) The Missouri Synod's original constitution expressly places the "administration of the ecclesiastical ordination and installation into the office" into the "sphere of business (*Geschaeftskreis*) of the Synod." (3) In 1874, and thus well within the life-time of

C.F.W. Walther. The Missouri Synod Convention resolved that the assembled Synod may by-pass the normal channels of electing teachers for synodical schools through their governing boards, since "the whole churchly power of the congregations is represented in the Synod when it is assembled" (1874 Report, p. 59).

Chicanery and tyranny are spawned not by the Synod's anchorage in the church's divine, evangelical, confessional "constitution", but precisely by a worldly-wise bureaucratic organizationalism wishing to cast aside churchly constraints.

And of course the church celebrates the Sacrament of the Altar only through its "regularly called" (ACXIV) local ministry — who may however do this not only in church-buildings, but also in prisons, hospitals, and barns, and therefore certainly also in seminary chapels. To recall Luther's Wittenberg again, the members of the theological faculty there did not float about in some Saxony-wide limbo, but were, quite locally, "ministers of the church in Wittenberg."

As for women voting in congregations, let me offer a few points which seem important to me, without in the least pretending that they solve the whole problem:

(1) Unlike the Roman Catholic and the Reformed churches, the Lutheran church knows of no divinely prescribed or "biblical" form of church government or external organization. So long as the pure Gospel and the Sacraments are safeguarded — which of course includes the presupposes the public ministry (not to be exercised by women) — external structure may differ from place to place, need not be ideal, and must not divide the church (AC V, VII , XIV, XXVIII). This relativizes all questions of external structure, including the place of "voting."

(2) A radical distinction must be made between voting in the State and in the Church. In modern democratic states, voting is indeed an exercise of sovereignty or authority, namely that of Rom. 13. But in the church it must "not be so" (St. Matt. 20:26). Only Christ has sovereignty and teaching authority in His church (St. Matt. 23:8). This authority belongs "immediately" (*Tractate*, 24) to the church, as a gift of her divine Bridegroom, and is publicly exercised through the public ministry. Where then is voting? Two cases are possible. Either the matter is settled in the written Word of God, and then voting exercises no authority but expresses either submission to and consensus in that Word (as crystallized in the church's orthodox confessions), or else opposition to it. Or, in the second case, the question is not decided in God's Word, and then neither majority nor minority but charity must rule, conscience may not be bound, and there should be an attitude of mutual yielding, not one of asserting "authority". (See Walther's magnificent *Pastoraltheologie*, 1897, pp.372-374).

(3) With reference to the application of the relevant biblical texts, different views are earnestly held within our Faculty, as within our Synod generally. But all the colleagues agree that this issue is not church-divisive. Let mutual respect prevail, and not an artificial uniformity.

Respectfully yours,

K . Marquart

cc: Robert Preus

Christian News, July 16, 1984

Editor's Note: The English translation of C. F. W. Walther's Pastoral Theology by John Drickamer was published by Christian News.

1. The "doctrine" of woman's suffrage is not one of the ____ before the Lutheran church.
2. The whole churchly power of the congregations is represented in the Synod when it is ____.
3. The church celebrates the Sacrament of the Altar only through ____.
4. Unlike the Roman Catholic and the Reformed churches, the Lutheran church knows of no divinely prescribed ____.

Index

108